AF615803

Student's Guide to the World Wide Web and WebCT

Deborah Morley
College of the Sequoias

Barb Solberg
Minot State University

Harcourt College Publishers
A Harcourt Higher Learning Company

Harcourt Integrated TechnologieS

ISBN: 0-03-045503-0

Copyright © 1999 by Harcourt Brace & Company

All rights reserved. No part of this publication may be reproduced or transmitted in any form or by any means, electronic or mechanical, including photocopy, recording, or any information storage and retrieval system, without permission in writing from the publisher.

Requests for permission to make copies of any part of the work should be mailed to:

Permissions Department
Harcourt, Inc.
6277 Sea Harbor Drive
Orlando, FL 32887-6777

Harcourt Integrated Technologies: A division of Harcourt College Publishers, A Harcourt Higher Learning Company

The WebCT logo on the cover is used by permission of WebCT.

Printed in the United States of America

PREFACE

Student's Guide to the World Wide Web and WebCT was designed for students using an online course in WebCT. This guide is the combination of two learning modules: *Introduction to the World Wide Web and Web Pages* by Deborah Morley and *Harcourt's Guide to WebCT* by Barb Solberg. This manual was designed to give the student a brief overview of the World Wide Web as well as a "how-to" manual for using WebCT's online tools. Divided into modules, this guide can serve as the starting point for students inexperienced with the Web or as a reference for more advanced students who can skip directly to the WebCT portion and begin their online course.

Using the World Wide Web (NET) module, students will learn about the origins of the Internet and the Web and will be introduced to such Internet basics as using a Web browser, creating bookmarks, downloading files, and sending and receiving e-mail. This section also details the elements of a Web page and explains how HTML and Web publishing programs can be used to create Web pages.

Using the WebCT (WCT) module, students will learn how to get started on their own computer using WebCT and will be introduced to the basics of WebCT course tools. This section also covers how to use the WebCT online communication tools, how to take online quizzes and exams, and how to monitor their progress.

Acknowledgements

I would like to thank Norm Friesen of the University of Alberta for reviewing this manual. Special thanks go to Steve Schoen, developmental editor, Cathy Spitzenberger, electronic publishing coordinator, Linda Beaupré, art director, and Renee Hopkins, editorial consultant, for their dedicated contributions.

Barb Solberg
Minot State University

CONTENTS

Internet and World Wide Web

Using WebCT

MODULE NET

Internet and World Wide Web

AFTER READING THIS MODULE, YOU WILL:

1. Understand how the Internet and World Wide Web originated and what they have evolved into today.
2. Understand how computers, computer users, and Web pages are identified on the Internet.
3. Be able to use a Web browser to explore the World Wide Web and to bookmark, save, and print Web pages.
4. Be able to use a Web browser to download files from the Internet.
5. Be able to use a Web browser to send and receive electronic mail.
6. Understand how Web pages may be created.

Introduction

A **computer network** is two or more computers connected together to share resources, such as hardware, software, and data. A network that covers a small geographical area, such as a room or a building, is called a **local area network** or **LAN.** A network that covers a larger geographical area is called a **wide area network** or **WAN.** Networks connected to other networks form an internet; the largest internet in the world is called the **Internet.** The Internet connects millions of computers all over the world.

This module will help you understand the history and current structure of the Internet and World Wide Web. You will learn how to use a Web browser to locate and view Web pages; how to print, save, and download information from the Internet; and how to send and receive electronic mail.

An internet set up by an organization that is accessed and used like the Internet, but which can only be accessed by authorized users of that organization, is called an INTRANET.

What Is the Internet and World Wide Web?

The Internet

The Internet originated from an experimental network called **ARPANET** created in 1969 by the U.S. Department of Defense's Advanced Research Projects Agency, or *ARPA.* The objective of ARPANET was to enable researchers located in different places to communicate with each other, as well as to create a network that could send data over a variety of paths to ensure that communications could continue even if part of the network was destroyed (presumably by war or natural disaster). Over the years, *protocols* (standards) were developed for transferring data over the network and for ensuring that the data were transferred intact. Other networks were soon connected to ARPANET, and eventually that internet evolved into the present-day Internet.

The number of computers continually connected to the Internet has grown at an extraordinary rate: from only four in 1969 to more than 20 million today.

In its early years, the Internet was used primarily by the government, scientists, and educational institutions, but today the Internet can be accessed by virtually anyone. Many people use the Internet daily to send and receive electronic mail, obtain product information, read newspaper and magazine articles, check the weather, get stock quotes, look up the address or telephone number of a company or individual, obtain government forms and documents, check airline schedules, and so forth. Though it was difficult to find information using the Internet in the past, the present-day Internet's numerous directories and search tools help users find the information that they are looking for.

One of the most remarkable characteristics of the Internet is that it is not owned by any person or organization, and no single person or organization is in charge. Each network connected to the Internet is managed individually by that organization's *network administrator,* but there is no network administrator for the Internet as a whole. The closest thing to an Internet governing body is a variety of organizations, such as the *Internet Society, Internet Architecture Board,* and *World Wide Web Consortium.* These organizations are involved with such issues as establishing the protocols or standards used on the Internet and encouraging cooperation and coordinating communication among the networks connected to the Internet.

Living room PCs (computers with large screen monitors, wireless keyboards, and television capabilities), _Internet access boxes_ that connect to a TV similar to a cable box and allow you to access the Internet through your existing television, and TVs and cellular phones with built-in Internet capabilities are integrating the home computer, the telephone, and the television and are expected to help Internet usage continue to increase in the near future.

The World Wide Web

The **World Wide Web** (also called the *Web, WWW,* or *W3)* is a collection of documents—called **Web pages**—accessed through the Internet. Web pages are located on computers continually connected to the Internet and are displayed with a software program called a **Web browser.** Web pages are connected together with **hyperlinks**—graphics or text that are clicked with the mouse to display other

Web pages. When a hyperlink is clicked, the appropriate Web page is displayed, whether that page belongs to the same organization and is on the same computer as the page containing the hyperlink, or belongs to a different organization located across the country or in a different country. Hyperlinks can also allow you to quickly jump around within a Web page, in addition to jumping you from page to page—much different from the linear, structured manner in which we are accustomed to reading books.

When the Web was developed in 1989 by scientists at the European Laboratory for Particle Physics (usually referred to as *CERN)* as a way for scientists to exchange documents over the Internet, Web pages contained only text and hyperlinks. In 1993, a group of professors and students at the University of Illinois National Center for Supercomputing Applications *(NCSA)* released *Mosaic,* the first graphically-based Web browser. Mosaic allowed Web pages to include graphical images in addition to text, and use of the World Wide Web increased dramatically. Today the Web is a true multimedia experience—Web pages can contain text, graphics, animation, sound, video, and three-dimensional virtual reality worlds.

A number of Web browsers are currently available to view Web pages, but the two most widely used are **Netscape Navigator** and **Microsoft Internet Explorer.** In addition to displaying Web pages, most browsers today can perform the functions of other Internet tools to access Internet resources other than the World Wide Web, such as electronic mail and collections of files. This capability has made the Web browser a universal tool for exploring and using the Internet. Some of the most common Internet tools are listed in Figure NET 1. Though these tools have been incorporated into many Web browsers, several of the tools—primarily electronic mail and FTP programs—are still frequently found as individual software programs.

The World Wide Web is the fastest-growing and most widely used Internet resource, consisting of millions of Web pages. Because the Web is so commonly used, many people use *Web* and *Internet* as interchangeable terms.

Exploring the Web by clicking on hyperlinks is often called *surfing the Web.*

FIGURE NET 1
Key Internet Tools

- *Web browsers*—allow you easy access to the World Wide Web and other Internet resources. The most common tool used to access the Internet.
- *Electronic mail*—allows you to send electronic messages to other Internet users.
- *File transfer protocol (FTP)*—allows you to transfer computer files (data files, software programs, etc.) between your computer and other computers on the Internet.
- *Gopher*—enables you to locate and retrieve Internet documents using a system of menus.
- *News groups/discussion groups*—allow you to post and read articles on a wide variety of subjects.
- *Telnet*—allows you to connect to and use another Internet computer as if you were directly connected (such as accessing a library electronic card catalog from home).
- *Conferencing/chat*—allows you to have real-time voice or typed conversations with other Internet users.

Accessing the Internet and World Wide Web

To access the Internet, you need a computer that is part of a network continually connected to the Internet (called a *direct connection)* or you need a **modem** (an interface board or other piece of hardware that connects your computer to your telephone line) to dial up and connect to a computer that is continually connected to the Internet (called a *dial-up connection).* The computer to which you connect is usually connected to a larger network called a *regional network;* regional networks are connected to the major high-speed networks within each country called *backbone networks.* Backbone networks within a country are connected together

Being connected to the Internet is often called being *online*.

When you are connected to the Internet using a modem, you will not be able to use your telephone or receive telephone calls unless you have more than one telephone line.

and to backbone networks in other countries to form one enormous network of networks—the Internet. An example of how a computer might be connected to the Internet is shown in Figure NET 2.

A computer that allows other computers to access the Internet is called a **host** computer. With a direct connection (most commonly used in schools and businesses), your computer always has access to its host computer; with a dial-up connection (most commonly used in homes), your modem dials and connects to a host computer belonging to a **commercial online service** or **Internet service provider (ISP),** companies that provide Internet access for a monthly fee. Commercial online services, such as *America Online* and *CompuServe,* provide a variety of services and activities, such as shopping, travel, children's activities, news, games, and so forth, in addition to Internet access. As shown in Figure NET 3a, commercial online services often use a unique interface that contains a built-in Web browser to access the World Wide Web when requested. Internet service providers, or ISPs, such as *The Microsoft Network, AT&T WorldNet, Prodigy Internet,* and numerous local companies, usually just connect you to the World Wide Web using Netscape Navigator or Microsoft Internet Explorer, as shown in Figure NET 3b, and don't usually provide many special services.

FIGURE NET 2

How an individual computer might be connected to the Internet.

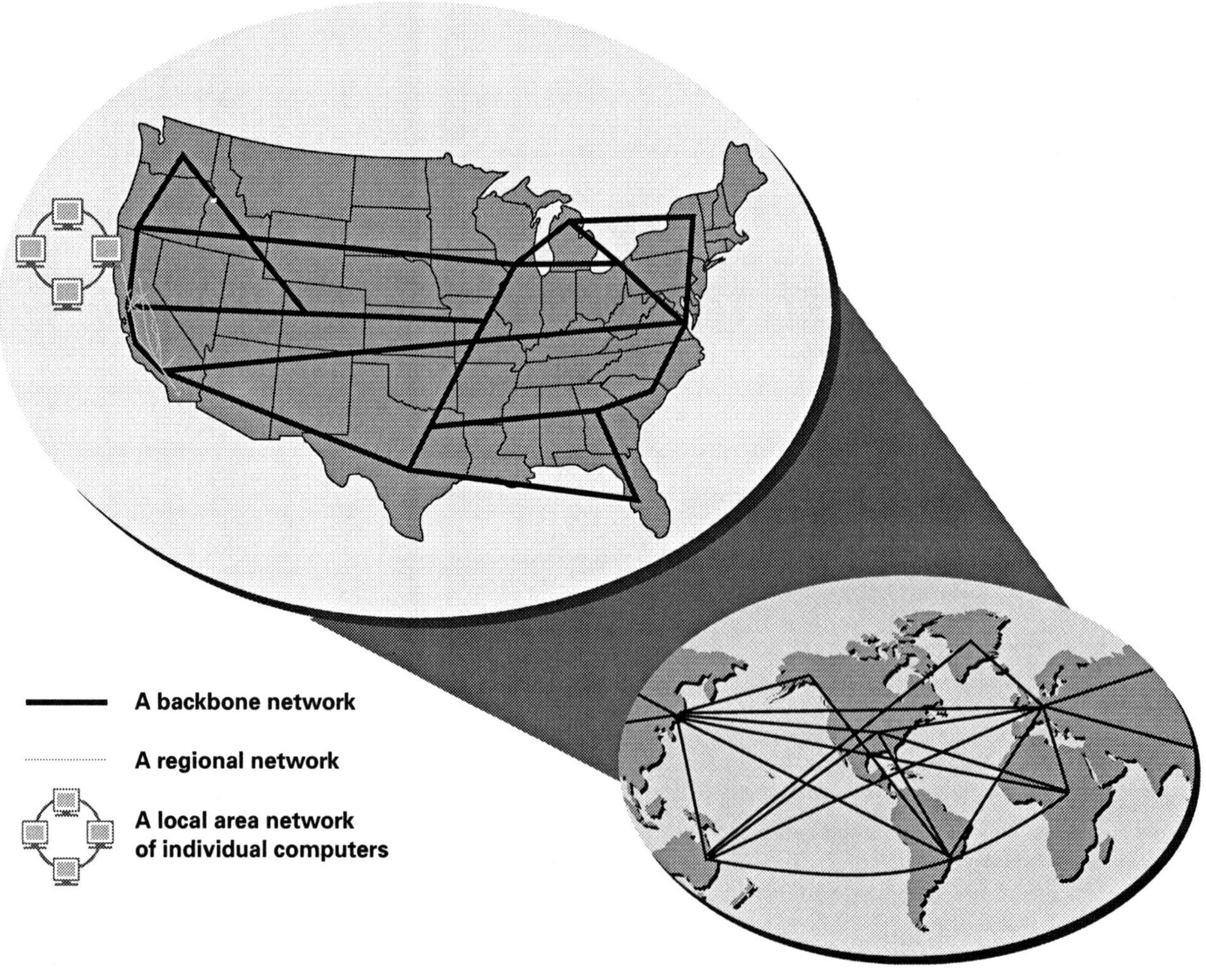

FIGURE NET 3

Commercial online services and Internet service providers.

Click to access the Internet using America Online's Web browser

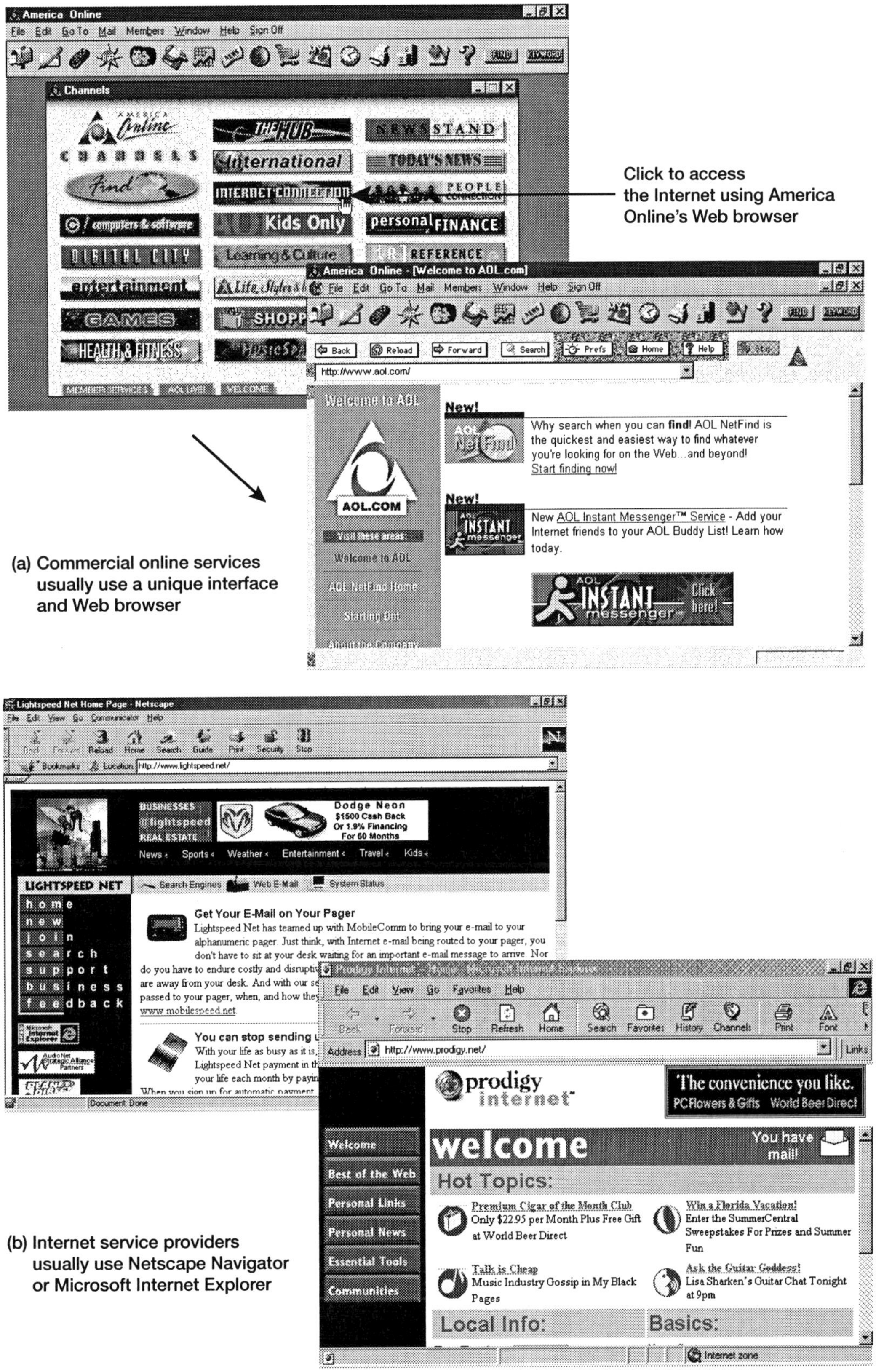

(a) Commercial online services usually use a unique interface and Web browser

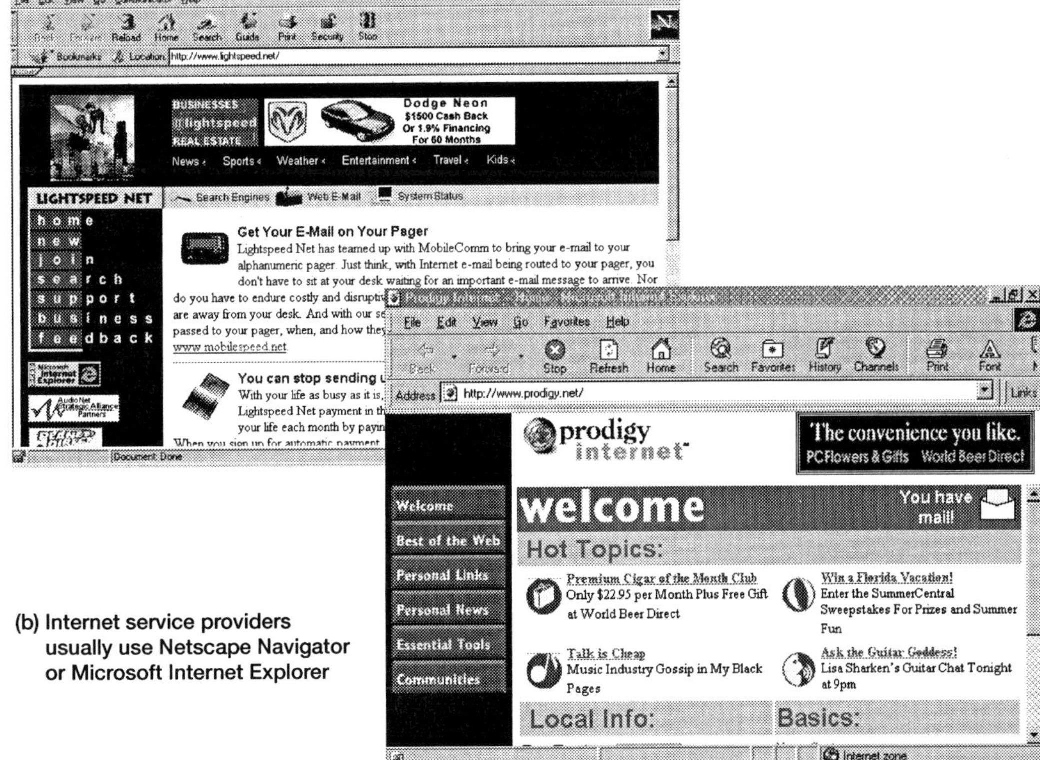

(b) Internet service providers usually use Netscape Navigator or Microsoft Internet Explorer

FIGURE NET 4

Connecting to the Internet.

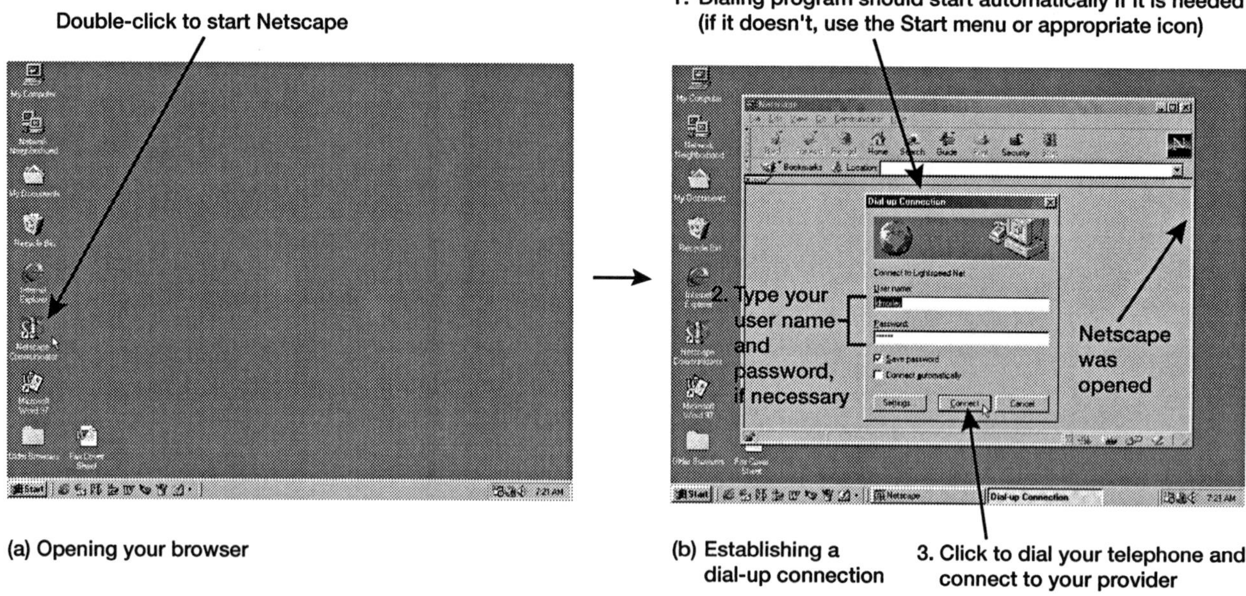

Many commercial online services and Internet service providers offer a free trial period. Before signing up, however, make sure that the provider has a local *access number* (the phone number that your computer will call to connect to the service) and watch for extra fee notices (not all features on a commercial online service are included in the monthly fee) to avoid unexpected charges. Many companies offer several pricing plans, such as a flat fee for an unlimited number of hours or a fee based on the number of hours online—select the pricing plan that best fits your needs and budget.

All types of Internet connections require at least one software program. With a direct connection, you will usually just need a Web browser program. With a dial-up connection, you will use either a special program supplied by your provider or a standard Web browser plus a second program (such as Windows' Dial-up Networking) to dial your modem. Once the necessary software has been installed on your computer and set up according to your provider's instructions, to access the Internet you only need to start the appropriate program using the Start menu or the appropriate desktop icon, as shown in Figure NET 4. Windows 98 will usually automatically start your dialing program if it is needed when the browser is opened; if it doesn't, start your dialing program using the Start menu or its desktop icon. You will then usually be asked to type your *user name* (a short identifying name that is often an abbreviation of your first and last name) and password before being connected to the Internet; user names and passwords are either assigned by your provider, network administrator, or are chosen during software installation.

Once you are connected to the Internet, you should either see the opening screen for your commercial online service from which you can usually select an option to access the World Wide Web when desired (as in Figure NET 3a), or a Web page already displayed in your browser (as in Figure NET 3b). To disconnect from the Internet, close your browser and any other program you opened to connect to the Internet. With a dial-up connection, you may be automatically disconnected or given the choice to close your telephone connection; if not, right-click on the icon on the right edge of the status bar and select *Disconnect* to hang up your telephone.

Internet Addresses

Computers, people, and Web pages are identified on the Internet and World Wide Web by unique **Internet addresses,** just as buildings and people have unique mailing addresses. A computer can be identified by its numerical *IP address* (usually used by other computers) or its text-based *domain name* (usually used by people); a person is identified by his or her *e-mail address;* and a Web page is identified by its *Uniform Resource Locator* (*URL*).

IP ADDRESSES AND DOMAIN NAMES

A network computer that contains information or software that other computers can request is called a **server;** the requesting computer is called the **client.** A server continually connected to the Internet to host Web pages is called a **Web server.** Each server that can be accessed through the Internet has a unique **IP address,** a numeric Internet address (such as *206.68.137.41).* Most of these computers also have a unique text-based address, called a **domain name** (such as *microsoft.com)* that corresponds to the computer's IP address. As shown in Figure NET 5, a domain name identifies the location of a computer; it can include the name of the computer, the appropriate department, school, business, geographical location, type of organization, etc. The parts of a domain name are separated by periods and listed with the most specific part first and the least specific part (the broadest category) listed last. The last part of a domain name (called the *top-level domain)* always describes a geographical location or type of organization. Seven of the original top-level domain names used in the United States and the seven new names introduced in 1997 and expected to be available sometime in 1998 are listed in Figure NET 6. Domains

> The speed of your modem (measured in bits per second or bps) greatly affects the speed of using the Internet. When buying a modem, be sure to buy one considered to be fast. At the time this book was written, a 28,800 bps modem—often referred to as a 28.8K modem—was a common speed, though most new computers were being sold with the faster 56K modem.

> The system used for translating domain names to IP addresses is called the *domain name system* or *DNS.*

> Domain names must be unique and are currently registered with an organization called *InterNIC.* To check whether a domain name is registered, or to obtain information about registering a domain name, visit the InterNIC Web site at *http://nic.internic.net*

FIGURE NET 5
IP address and domain name for College of the Sequoias.

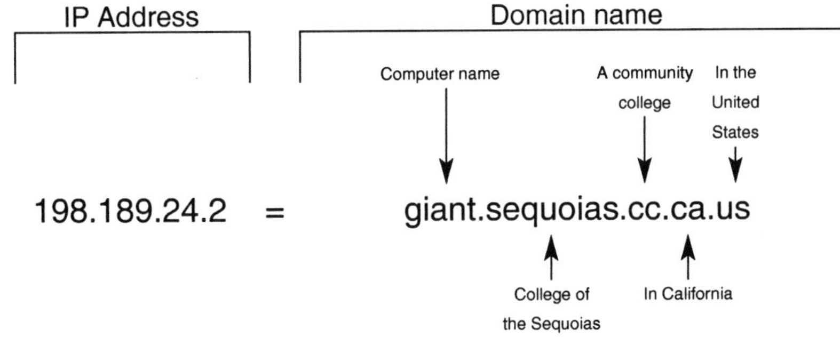

FIGURE NET 6
Top-level domains used in the United States.

	DOMAIN	TYPE OF ORGANIZATION
Original Domains	*.edu*	Educational institutions
	.gov	Government agenices
	.mil	Military
	.com	Commercial businesses
	.net	Network providers
	.org	Noncommercial organizations
	.us	United States
New Domains Created in 1997 (expected to be available in 1998)	*.firm*	Businesses
	.store	Businesses offering goods to purchase
	.web	Organizations emphasizing activitites related to the World Wide Web
	.arts	Organizations emphasizing activities related to the arts
	.rec	Organizations emphasizing recreation or entertainment
	.info	Organizations providing information services
	.nom	Individuals

Domain names are usually typed in lowercase and can only contain letters, numbers, and the hypen character (-); no spaces are allowed.

used outside of the United States usually identify the country where the server is located, such as *.fr* for France or *.uk* for the United Kingdom.

The domain name for College of the Sequoias shown in Figure NET 5 is longer than most; more typical domain names are shown in Figure NET 7.

FIGURE NET 7
Sample domain names.

DOMAIN NAME	ORGANIZATION	TYPE OF ORGANIZATION
berkeley.edu	UC Berkeley	Educational institution
microsoft.com	Microsoft Corporation	Commercial business
fbi.gov	Federal Bureau of Investigation	Government organization

E-MAIL ADDRESSES

To send or receive *electronic mail* (electronic messages usually referred to as *e-mail)* over the Internet, a person needs an **e-mail address.** E-mail addresses usually consist of the person's user name, followed by the @ symbol, followed by their computer's domain name (such as *deborahm@giant.sequoias.cc.ca.us).* E-mail addresses uniquely identify people on the Internet, just as a person's name combined with his or her street address gives that individual a unique mailing address.

One of the most fascinating aspects of the Internet is that, because of the protocols used, all computers on the Internet regardless of their type (IBM, Mac, etc.) or operating system (DOS, Windows, Unix, Mac OS, etc.) can view the same Web pages and exchange information.

UNIFORM RESOURCE LOCATORS (URLS)

Each page on the World Wide Web has a unique **Uniform Resource Locator,** or **URL** (sometimes pronounced *earl),* that identifies the name of the page and where it is located. The first part of an URL identifies the protocol being used followed by a colon and two forwards slashes, almost always *http://* for Web pages since most Web pages use *Hypertext Transfer Protocol* or *HTTP* (other possible protocols are *ftp://, gopher://, news://,* and *telnet://).* The second part of an URL identifies the server where the Web page is located. The third part of an URL identifies the location of the Web page on that computer, if necessary, with folder names and the appropriate filename separated by forward slashes. Two sample URLs are shown in Figure NET 8.

FIGURE NET 8
Sample URLs.

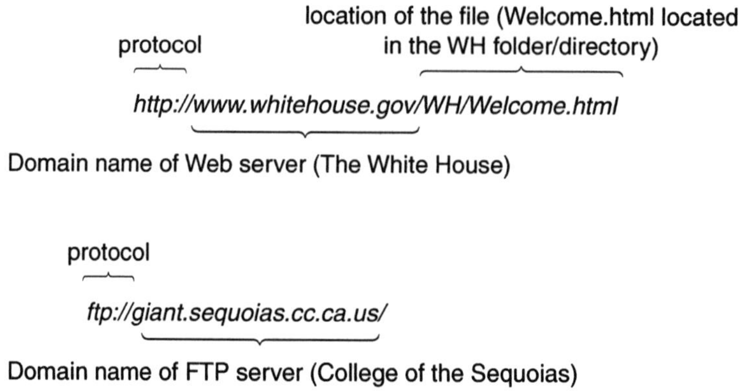

PRONOUNCING INTERNET ADDRESSES

Because Internet addresses are frequently given verbally, it is important to know how to pronounce them. Here are a few guidelines:

- If a portion of the address forms a recognizable word or name, it is spoken; otherwise it is spelled out.
- The @ sign is pronounced *at.*
- The period (.) is pronounced *dot.*
- The forward slash (/) is pronounced *slash.*

Some sample Internet addresses and their pronunciations are shown in Figure NET 9.

FIGURE NET 9
Sample Internet addresses and their pronunciations.

ADDRESS	PRONOUNCED AS
berkeley.edu	berkeley dot e d u
president@whitehouse.gov	president at whitehouse dot gov
deborahm@giant.sequoias.cc.ca.us	deborah m at giant dot sequoias dot c c dot c a dot u s
microsoft.com/IE/Intro.htm	microsoft dot com slash i e slash Intro dot h t m

Browsing the World Wide Web

As mentioned previously, the two most widely used Web browsers at the present time are Netscape Navigator and Microsoft Internet Explorer. Web browsers generally look and act very similarly; after you know how to use one, you will easily be able to use others. This textbook alternates between displaying screens using Netscape Navigator version 4.0 and Microsoft Internet Explorer version 4.0. If you have a different version of one of these browsers or are using a different browser altogether, the screens in this textbook will probably look a little different than yours, but they should be close enough for you to understand how the concepts relate to your browser.

There are a number of interesting Web sites to visit in the "Web Sites for Students" in the Appendix of this text.

When you first connect to the World Wide Web using a Web browser, you see the **home page** or starting page for your browser's **Web site**—a group of Web pages that belong together and are usually stored in the same location on a server, such as all the pages for a company or department. (If you see a different Web page, such as your school's home page, your browser has been set up to display a different initial page.) Figure NET 10 illustrates the Netscape Navigator and Microsoft Internet Explorer browsers with their corresponding home pages displayed.

Parts of the Browser Window

As shown in Figure NET 10, browser windows contain special browsing buttons and indicators in addition to the standard Windows components, such as the title bar, menu bar, scroll bar, and so forth.

COMMAND TOOLBAR

Both Navigator and Internet Explorer have a **command toolbar** located below the menu bar that enables you to quickly access the most frequently used

FIGURE NET 10
Parts of a browser window.

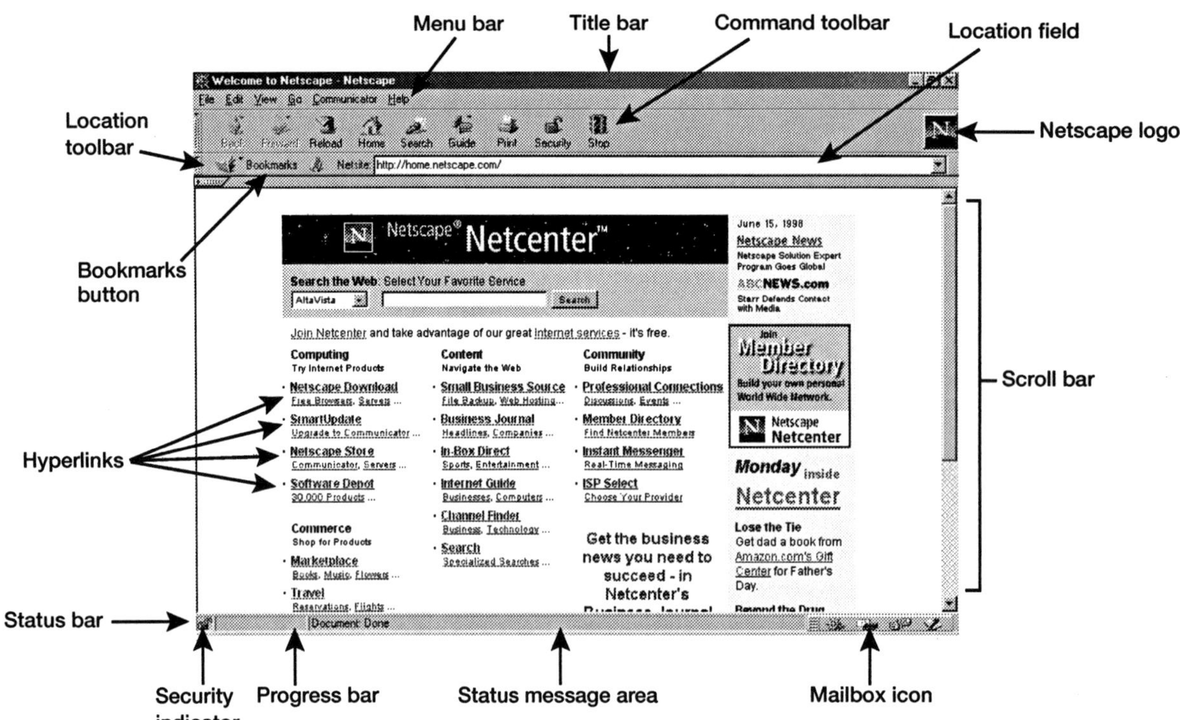

(a) Netscape Navigator

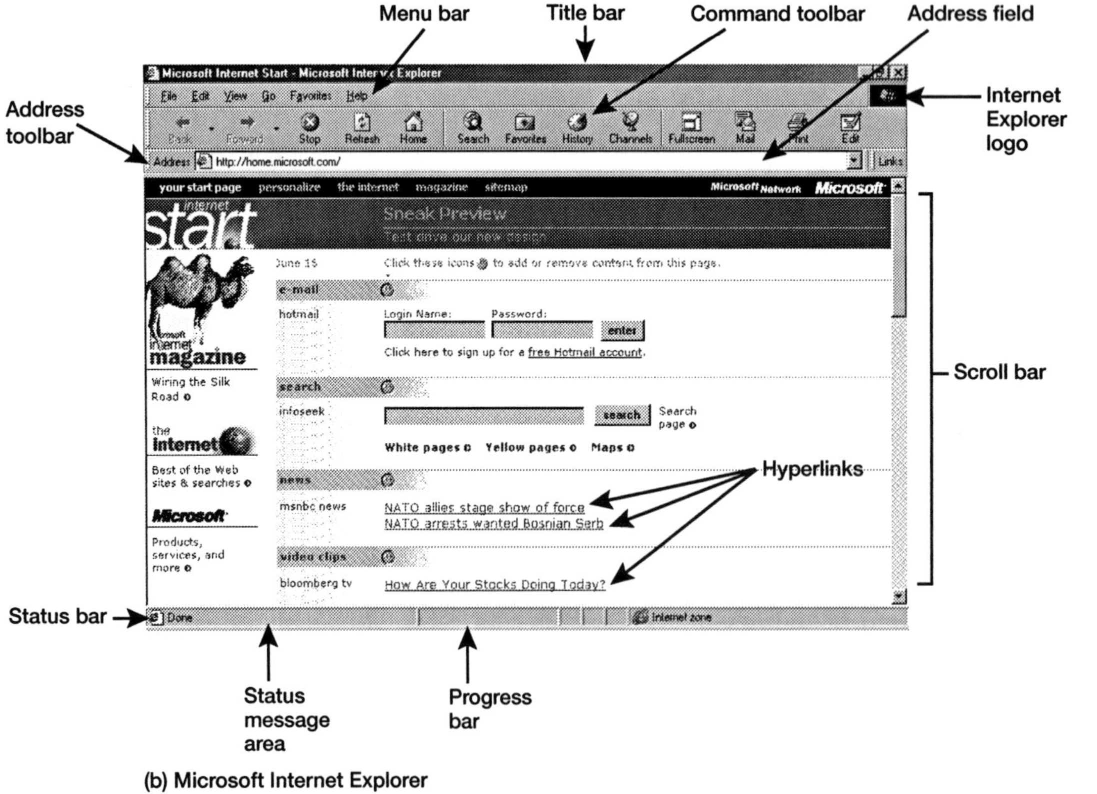

(b) Microsoft Internet Explorer

browser commands. The most commonly used command toolbar buttons are described next.

- *Back* is used to move back to a page that has already been displayed during the current Internet session. (When this button is dim, you have no previous pages, and the button is unavailable.)
- *Forward* is used to move forward again after using the Back button to move to a previous page. (When this button is dim, you have not moved backwards yet, and the button is unavailable.)
- *Home* displays the established initial page for your browser—usually the home page for your browser or for your commercial online service or Internet service provider.
- *Search* displays options for searching for specific Web pages, e-mail addresses, and other information.
- *Print* allows you to print the page that is currently displayed.
- *Stop* stops the transfer of a page while it is being loaded (useful when a page is taking a long time to display). Once the page has loaded (indicated in Navigator by the Stop button no longer being red), the Stop button is unavailable.
- *Reload* or *Refresh* redisplays the current page (useful if an error prevented the page from loading properly or you want to reload a page that changes frequently).

LOCATION/ADDRESS TOOLBAR

Below the command toolbar is an additional toolbar called the **location toolbar** in Navigator and the **address toolbar** in Internet Explorer. As shown in Figure NET 10, this toolbar contains a white rectangle called the **location field** or **address field** where URLs can be typed to go directly to specific Web pages (typing URLs will be discussed later in this module). The Navigator location toolbar also contains a *Bookmarks* button that can be used to return to favorite Web pages; Internet Explorer has a similar *Favorites* button on its command toolbar (using bookmarks will also be discussed later in this module).

STATUS BAR

As shown in Figure NET 10, the **status bar** is located at the bottom of each browser window. The status bar's *progress bar* fills up as a page is being loaded to indicate how much of the transfer has been completed. Next to the progress bar is the *status message area,* which provides information about the transfer as a page is being loaded. On the right edge of the status bar is an area for icons: Navigator displays icons that enable you to switch between the Navigator window and other windows, such as the Messenger window for e-mail; Internet Explorer displays the *Internet zone* icon while you are accessing the Internet (it displays other icons when you are accessing other resources, such as *My Computer* when you are viewing a file located on your computer) and adds additional icons, such as a security icon to indicate a secure page, when necessary.

Moving through the World Wide Web

USING URLS

As mentioned earlier in this module, URL is an abbreviation for Uniform Resource Locator—a Web page's address. Since it has become very common to see URLs listed in television and print advertisements, magazine and newspaper

When using a screen resolution of 640x480, not all of Internet Explorer's toolbar buttons will be visible on the screen. When you need access to the Print button and other buttons located on the right edge of the toolbar in this resolution, click the *Fullscreen* toolbar button to display all of the command toolbar buttons (click the Fullscreen button again to return to the original display).

The security indicators on a browser's status bar tell you if the Web page you are currently viewing is secure for transferring sensitive information (such as a credit card number), so that the information can't easily be intercepted by other Internet users. A locked padlock on the status bar indicates a secure page; Navigator displays an unlocked padlock (as in Figure NET 10a) when the page is not secure.

Recent versions of both Navigator and Internet Explorer keep track of recently visited URLs and try to complete each URL as you type it—if it finishes typing the correct URL for you, just press Enter to load that page. You can also select a recent URL by clicking on the ▾ button at the right edge of the location/address field or going to the History list available through the Internet Explorer toolbar or the Navigator menu bar. To select a page visited during the current session, click on the down arrow on Internet Explorer's Back and Forward buttons or click on Navigator's Go menu.

Text hyperlinks (called *hypertext)* usually appear on Web pages as underlined, blue text, as shown in Figure NET 10. If you are not sure if a word or an image on a Web page is a hyperlink, rest the mouse pointer on it for a moment. If the pointer turns into a pointing hand, it is a hyperlink.

Hypertext links that you have used (called *followed links)* usually remain a different color to help you keep track of where you have been. How long the followed links remain a different color depends on how your browser is set up on your computer.

articles, radio and news broadcasts, on business cards, and so forth, it is important to know how to access a particular Web page using its URL.

To move to a Web page using its URL, click in the location/address field and type the appropriate URL (you can either edit the existing URL or delete it and type the new one)—be sure to match the spelling, case, and punctuation exactly. For example, to move to the "U.S. Postal Service ZIP Code" Web page, type the URL *http://www.usps.gov/ncsc* as shown in Figure NET 11a (most Web browsers will allow you to leave off the *http://* when typing an URL). After typing the URL, press Enter and the appropriate page will appear, as shown in Figure NET 11b.

USING HYPERLINKS

To move to new Web pages using hyperlinks, just click on the appropriate hyperlink with the mouse. For example, to move to the "U.S. Postal Service ZIP+4 Code Lookup" Web page from the page displayed in Figure NET 11b, move the mouse pointer to the underlined words *ZIP+4 Code Lookup,* as shown in Figure NET 12a. The mouse pointer will turn into a pointing hand to indicate that you are pointing to a hyperlink, and the corresponding URL will appear in the status message area. After pointing to the hyperlink, click once with the mouse to make the appropriate page appear, as shown in Figure NET 12b.

USING BOOKMARKS

Once you have located an interesting Web page, you can save its URL to allow you to return to that page easily—a process called creating a **bookmark** or adding a page to your list of **favorites.** To create a bookmark for a particular Web

FIGURE NET 11
Typing an URL to move to a new Web page.

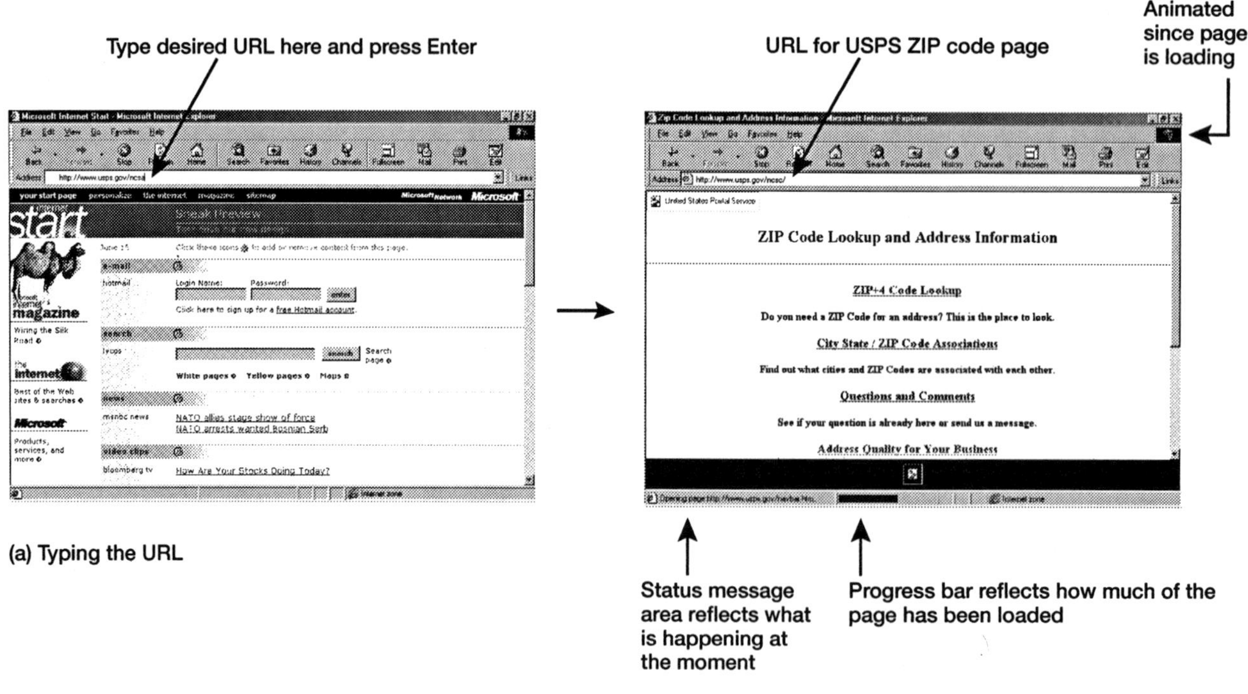

(a) Typing the URL

(b) The new Web page appears

FIGURE NET 12
Using a hyperlink to move to a new Web page.

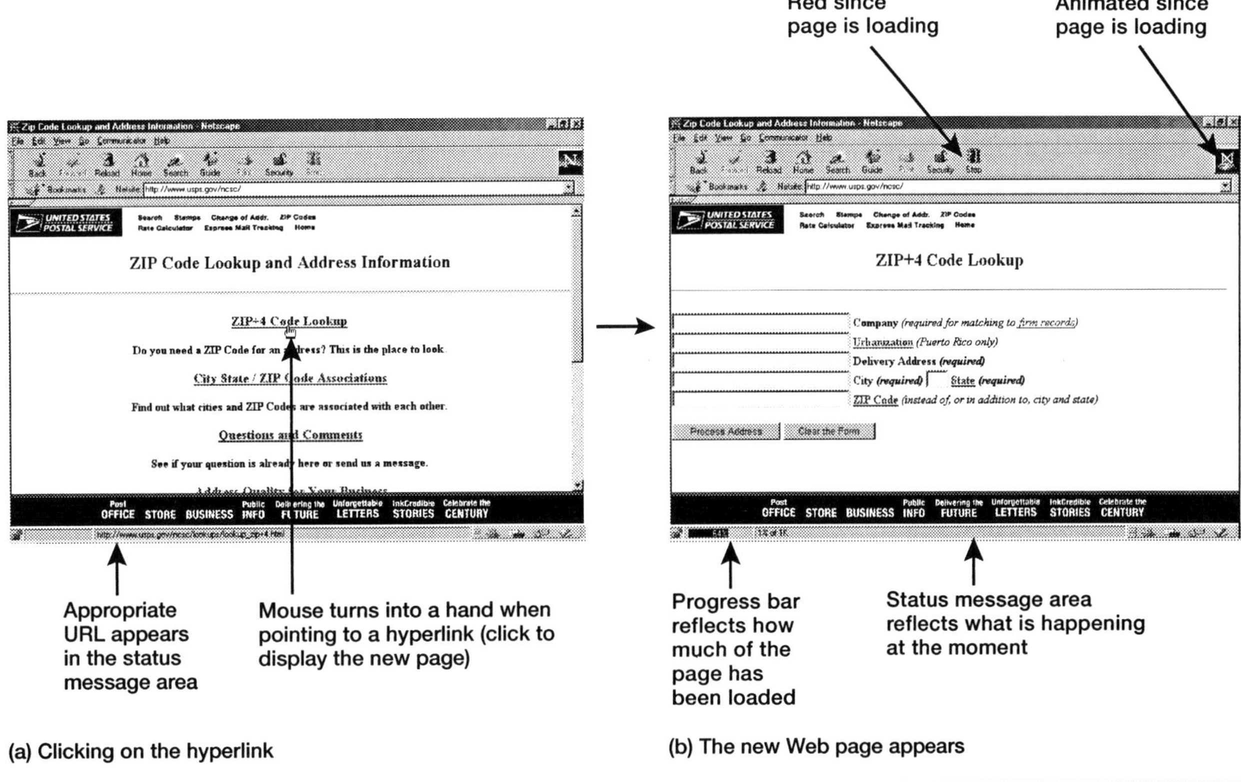

(a) Clicking on the hyperlink

(b) The new Web page appears

page using Internet Explorer, go to that page, then select *Add to Favorites* from the Favorites menu, as shown in Figure NET 13a, then click *OK* on the dialog box displayed to add that page to your list of favorites (select one of the other options if you would like to *subscribe* to the Web page to receive notification or have the Web page automatically downloaded to your computer when the content changes). (Netscape users: Click on the Bookmarks button and select *Add Bookmark* instead or select *File Bookmark* to store the bookmark in an existing folder—see the Bookmarks menu in Figure NET 14a.) The bookmark will be displayed when you click on the Favorites menu or Bookmarks button from that point on, as shown in Figure NET 13b. To go to a page for which you have made a bookmark, just click on the appropriate bookmark in the list.

Bookmarks are usually saved on the hard drive of the computer on which you are working and are always available when your browser is open. This is fine if you are working on your own personal computer at home or at work, but if you are working in a computer lab where you share a computer with other people, usually everyone's bookmarks will be stored together in the same bookmark file on that computer, making the bookmark list large and disorganized. If you are sharing a computer and would like to keep your own personal bookmarks, Navigator allows you to save them to a floppy disk and retrieve them when necessary during future sessions (Internet Explorer doesn't support this feature yet, though you can copy your personal Favorites folder back and forth between your floppy disk and hard drive using Windows Explorer). To save your bookmarks onto a floppy disk using Navigator (shown in Figure NET 14):

It is common to receive an error message such as *Unable to locate the server* or *The server doesn't have a DNS entry* when you are trying to move to a new Web page. If you get an error when typing a URL, you may have made a typographical error; if so, correct it and try it again. If you still receive an error, or if you receive an error when clicking on a hyperlink, the computer hosting the page may be busy (if so, press Enter to try again or try the page again later), or the page may have been moved or deleted (if so, try shortening the URL to eliminate folder and filenames to try to display the home page of that Web site; you can then attempt to get to the desired page from there).

FIGURE NET 13
Adding and using a bookmark or list of favorites.

1. Click to add the current page to the favorites list

Folders originally created by Internet Explorer

2. Select the desired option

3. Click to add the page

(a) Adding a bookmark

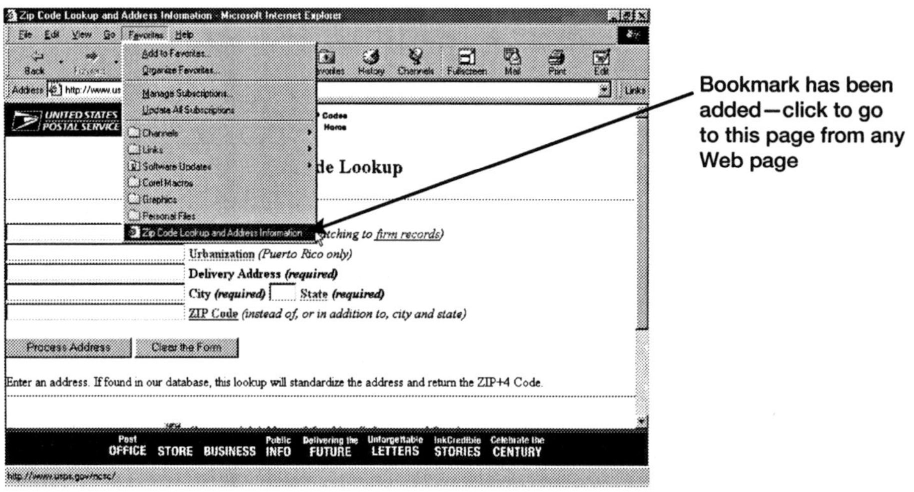

(b) Using the bookmark

It is easy to lose track of time when you are on the Internet. Be sure to watch the clock closely (set a timer if necessary) to budget your online time.

1. Insert a disk into your floppy drive.
2. Click on the Bookmarks button and select *Edit Bookmarks* to go to the Bookmarks window (Figure NET 14a).
3. Select *Save As* from the Bookmarks window File menu, then change the save location to your floppy drive, type the desired filename for the bookmarks file, and click *Save* to save the file (Figure NET 14b).

To open the bookmarks file from your floppy disk in Navigator, click on the Bookmarks button and select *Edit Bookmarks* to go to the Bookmarks window, then select *Open Bookmarks File* from the File menu and select your bookmarks file. The Bookmarks window also allows you to create folders to keep your bookmarks organized—you can create new folders, drag bookmarks into

FIGURE NET 14

Saving the bookmark file to a floppy disk.

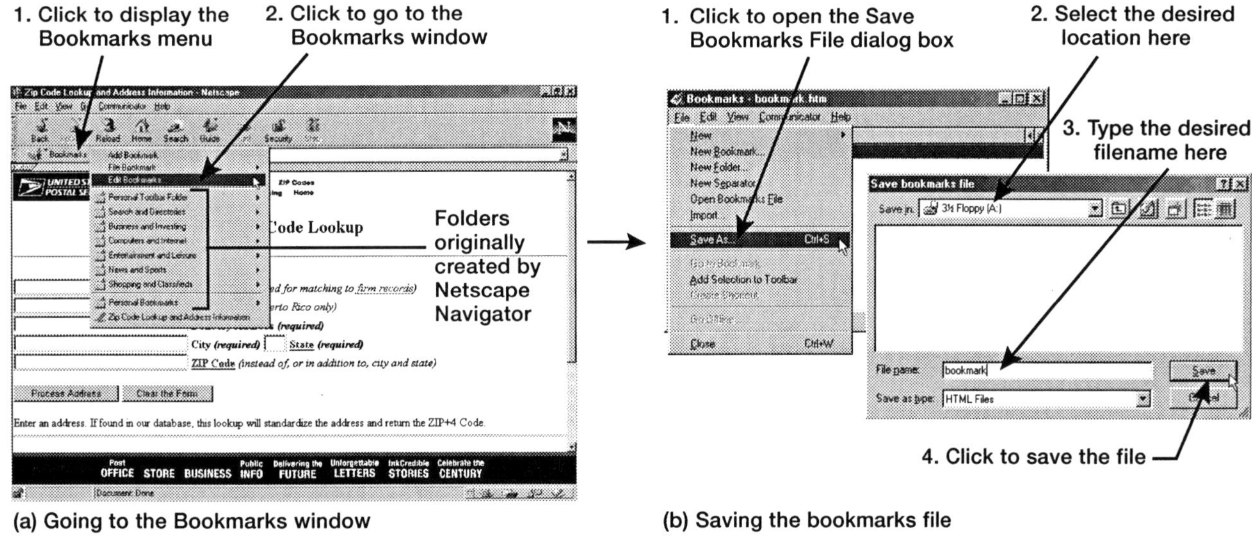

the appropriate folders with the mouse, or delete bookmarks by selecting the bookmarks to be deleted and pressing the Delete key on the keyboard. (Internet Explorer users: Select *Organize Favorites* from the Favorites menu to get to a similar screen to organize your bookmarks.)

Searching the World Wide Web

Exploring the Web can be very time-consuming, especially if you are looking for something specific. There are a number of special Web pages, called **search sites,** available to help you locate what you are looking for on the Internet.

Both Netscape and Internet Explorer have an online guide to the Web to help you find sites in particular categories. In Netscape, click the *Guide* toolbar button; in Internet Explorer, click the *Channels* toolbar button.

A search site uses a **search engine,** a **directory,** or both to locate Web pages that meet your search criteria. A search engine is a software program that allows you to type in one or more key words, then the search engine searches a previously created database of Web pages to find and display a list of Web pages that meet your criteria. A directory organizes Web pages into categories; to find Web pages on a particular topic, click on appropriate categories until you find a list of Web pages that match your chosen topic.

To begin a search, either click on the Search button [Search] or [Search] on your browser's toolbar or type the URL for a search site in the location/address field. An illustration of searching for clip art using the Infoseek search site is shown in Figure NET 15. Some general search tips are listed in Figure NET 16.

Printing and Saving Web Pages

When you find a Web page that contains useful or interesting information, you may want to either print the page or save some of the information on the page to read or print later. Be careful when using information from a Web site, however, as the content and images located on Web pages are copyrighted unless otherwise specified. You should credit all Web sources appropriately, and don't include any text or images obtained from other Web pages on your own Web site without first obtaining permission from the author of the site. Use the e-mail link located on a

FIGURE NET 15
Using a search site that utilizes both a search engine and a directory.

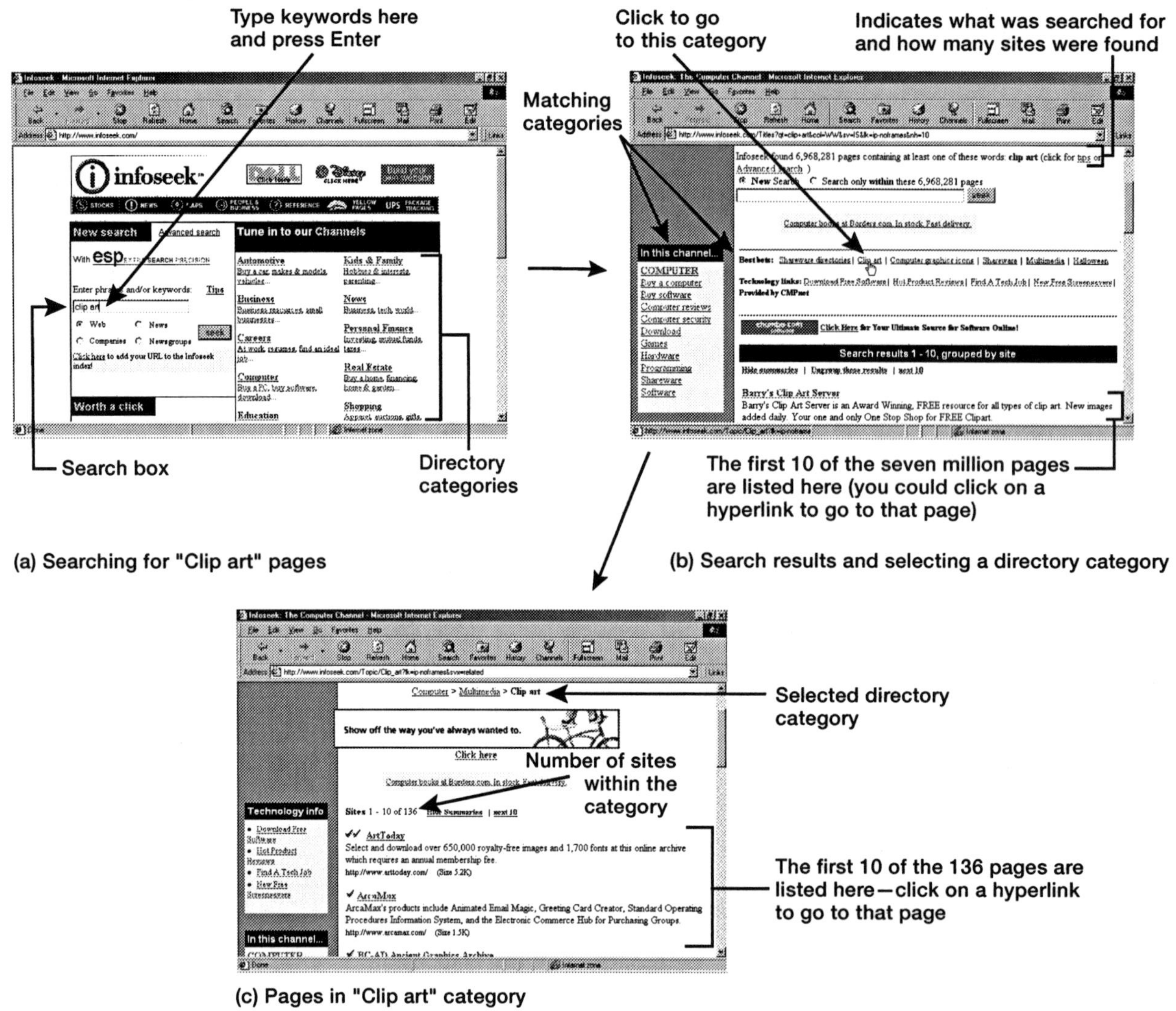

(a) Searching for "Clip art" pages

(b) Search results and selecting a directory category

(c) Pages in "Clip art" category

FIGURE NET 16
Tips for using search sites and directories.

- Select directory topics to find information on a general topic; type keywords to search for information about a specific topic.
- Before using a search site for the first time, read the search tips or instructions to see what search options are available.
- Try to be as specific as possible when typing keywords. Whenever possible, use more than one keyword and use appropriate operators (often + or quotation marks or the words "AND" or "NOT"—check the search tips to see the options available for the search site you are using) to specify exactly the pages that you want to see. You can usually use operators to specify to see just the pages containing all of the keywords, or pages containing any of the keywords, or pages containing some keywords but not others.
- If your search returns numerous hits and you can think of more specific keywords or a way to use operators to further limit your search, go back and redo the search to save time.
- If your search is not successful, try using other words that might locate the same information. For example, if you are searching for information about trends in computer use, you might try *trends computer use, computer use demographics, computer use statistics,* and so forth.
- Use more than one search site or directory—they often return surprisingly different hits.

Web page to ask about the conditions for use for any text or images you would like to use.

> **To determine how much of a Web page to print, use the *Print Preview* option of Netscape Navigator's File menu to preview the document. Then click Netscape's Print toolbar button to open the Print dialog box, and select the desired pages to print using the Pages *from:* and *to:* boxes. (Internet Explorer doesn't have a print preview option, though its Print dialog box does include *from:* and *to:* boxes to print individual pages when desired.)**

PRINTING A WEB PAGE

To print a Web page, select *Print* from the File menu or click on the Print toolbar button [Print] or [Print]. Netscape Navigator will display a Print dialog box—complete it and press the OK button to print the Web page. Internet Explorer only displays the Print dialog box when *Print* is selected from the File menu, and clicking the Print toolbar button will automatically print the entire Web page. When a Web page is divided into *frames* (separate areas each containing a separate Web page, as in Figure NET 17), the Print command usually only prints the current frame, so be sure you are in the proper frame (by clicking in it) before executing the Print command. Internet Explorer 4.0 allows you to print a page displayed in frames just as it looks on the screen—open your browser's Print dialog box to see if you have access to that option.

SAVING A WEB PAGE

To save information displayed on a Web page, you can either save the entire Web page using the File menu or you can copy some of the text to a word processor or other Windows program. When you save an entire Web page, the suggested file

FIGURE NET 17
Saving a Web page's text to a floppy disk.

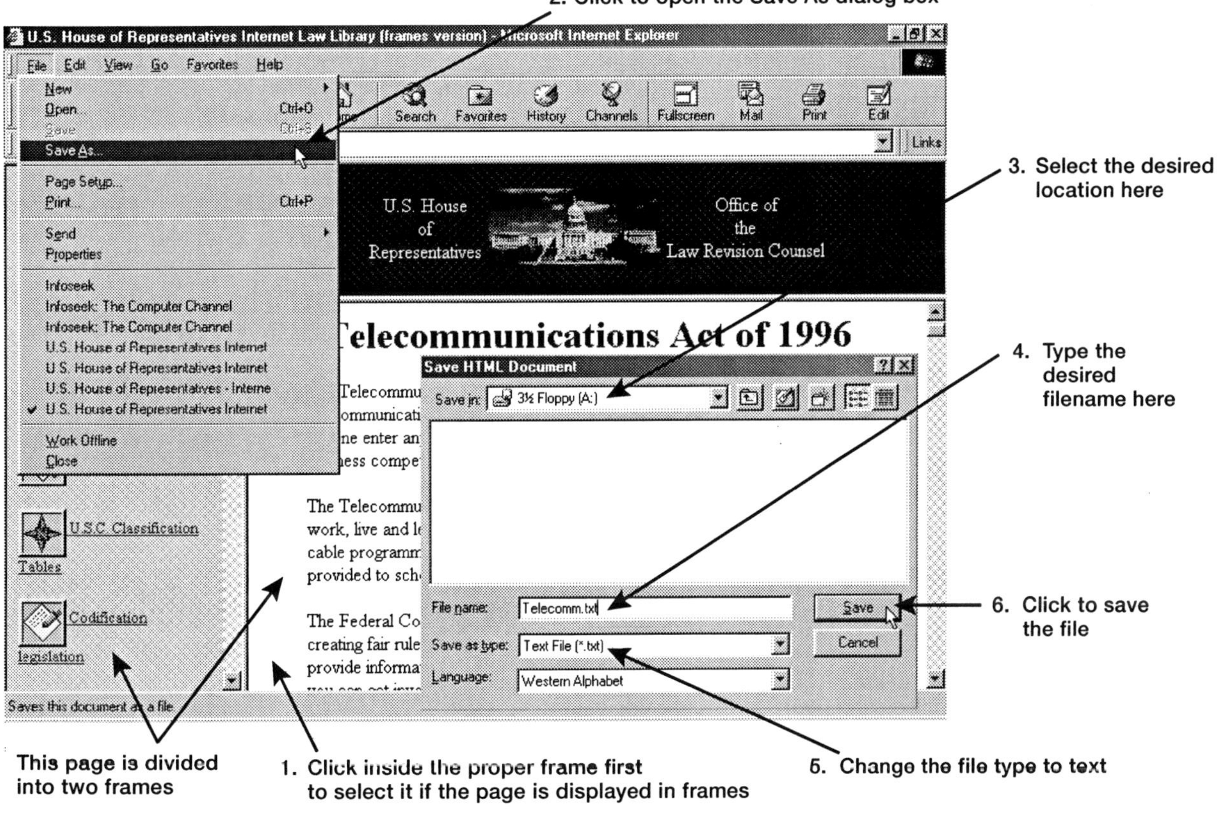

Information on a Web page is entered by the person or organization who created or is maintaining the page, so it is not always accurate. Try to verify any information that you want to use and consider the source—information from the government, research agencies, educational institutions, or the company or organization in question is usually more reliable than that from an individual's Web site.

type is the page's native HTML format which can be viewed using a Web browser. If you prefer, you can save the Web page in a plain text format that can be opened with any text editor or word processing program. To save the current Web page as plain text to a floppy disk (shown in Figure NET 17):

1. Insert a floppy disk into your floppy drive.
2. If the page is displayed in frames (as in Figure NET 17), click inside the desired frame to select it, since only the text in the current frame will be saved.
3. Use the *Save As* option of the File menu to bring up the Save As dialog box.
4. At the Save As dialog box, change the *Save in:* location to your floppy drive and type the desired filename using the extension *.txt.* Change the file type to *Plain Text (*.txt)* or *Text File (*.txt)* so that it can be retrieved in a text editor or word processing program, then click *Save* to save the file.

To copy the text from a Web page to a text editor or word processing program (shown in Figure NET 18):

FIGURE NET 18
Copying text from a Web page to a WordPad document.

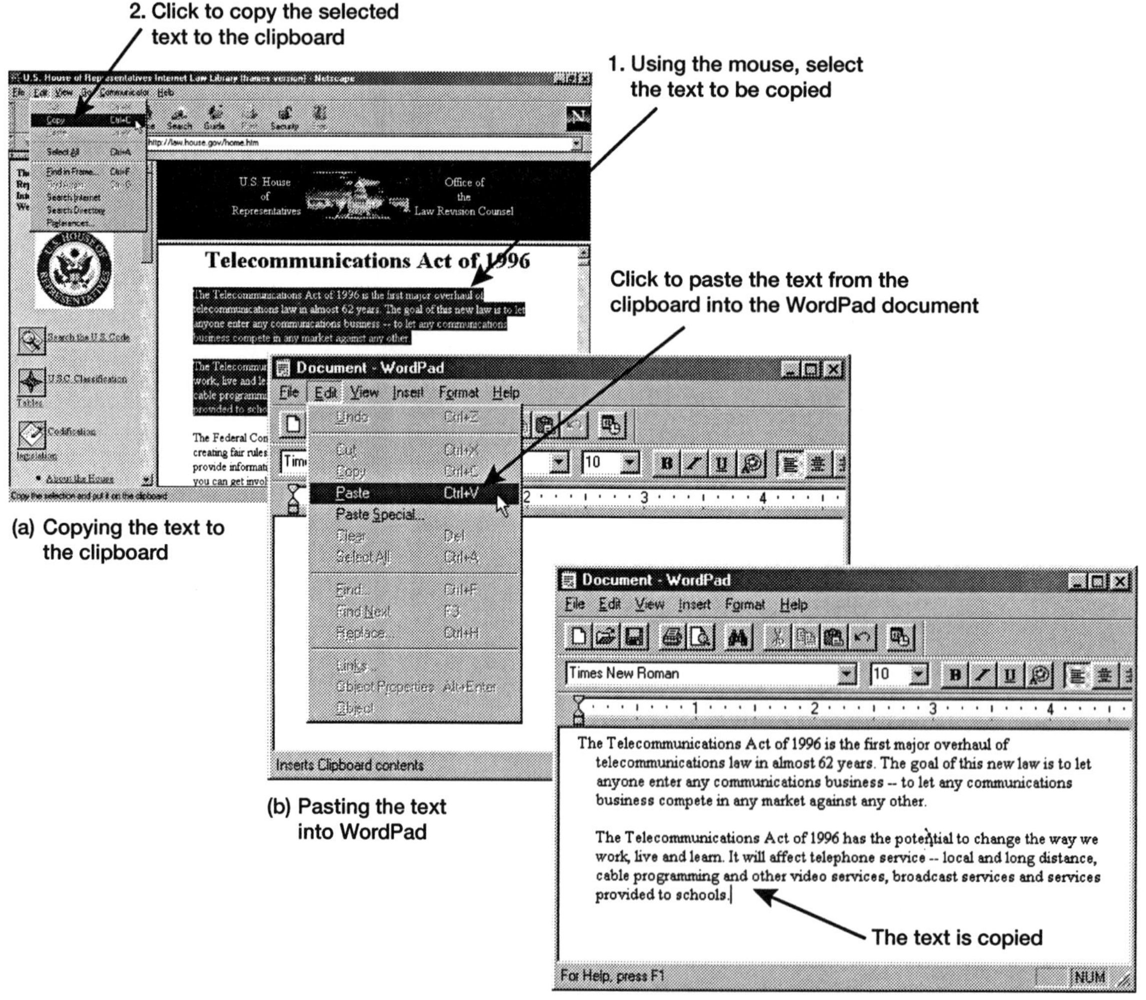

1. Using the mouse, select (highlight) the text to be copied, then choose *Copy* from the Edit menu to copy the text to the Windows *clipboard* (a central temporary holding place for Windows applications). (Figure NET 18a)
2. Open your word processing program and select *Paste* from the Edit menu to retrieve the text. (Figure NET 18b)
3. The text will then be inserted into the current document and can be edited, saved, and/or printed as usual. (Figure NET 18c)

Many software programs that you can download from the Internet are called *freeware* or *shareware* programs. Freeware programs can be downloaded and used for personal use without charge; shareware programs can be downloaded and used without charge for a trial period only. With shareware programs, at the end of the trial period you must either send payment to the author or erase the program from your computer.

Downloading Files from the Internet

When you are exploring the Web, it is common to run across a Web page that contains a hyperlink for **downloading** (copying) a file to your computer. Types of files that are commonly downloaded are software programs, government documents and forms, press releases, clip art images, and so forth. The protocol or standard often used to download a file is called **File Transfer Protocol** or **FTP.** Files can be downloaded by clicking on a hyperlink located on a Web page, as shown in Figure NET 19a, or by clicking on a hyperlink on an *FTP site* or *FTP server* (a computer that hosts files to be downloaded), as shown in Figure NET 19b. (Notice that the URL for the FTP server begins with *ftp://* instead of *http://.)* With either method, after clicking on the appropriate hyperlink you will need to complete the Save As

FIGURE NET 19

Downloading files from the Internet.

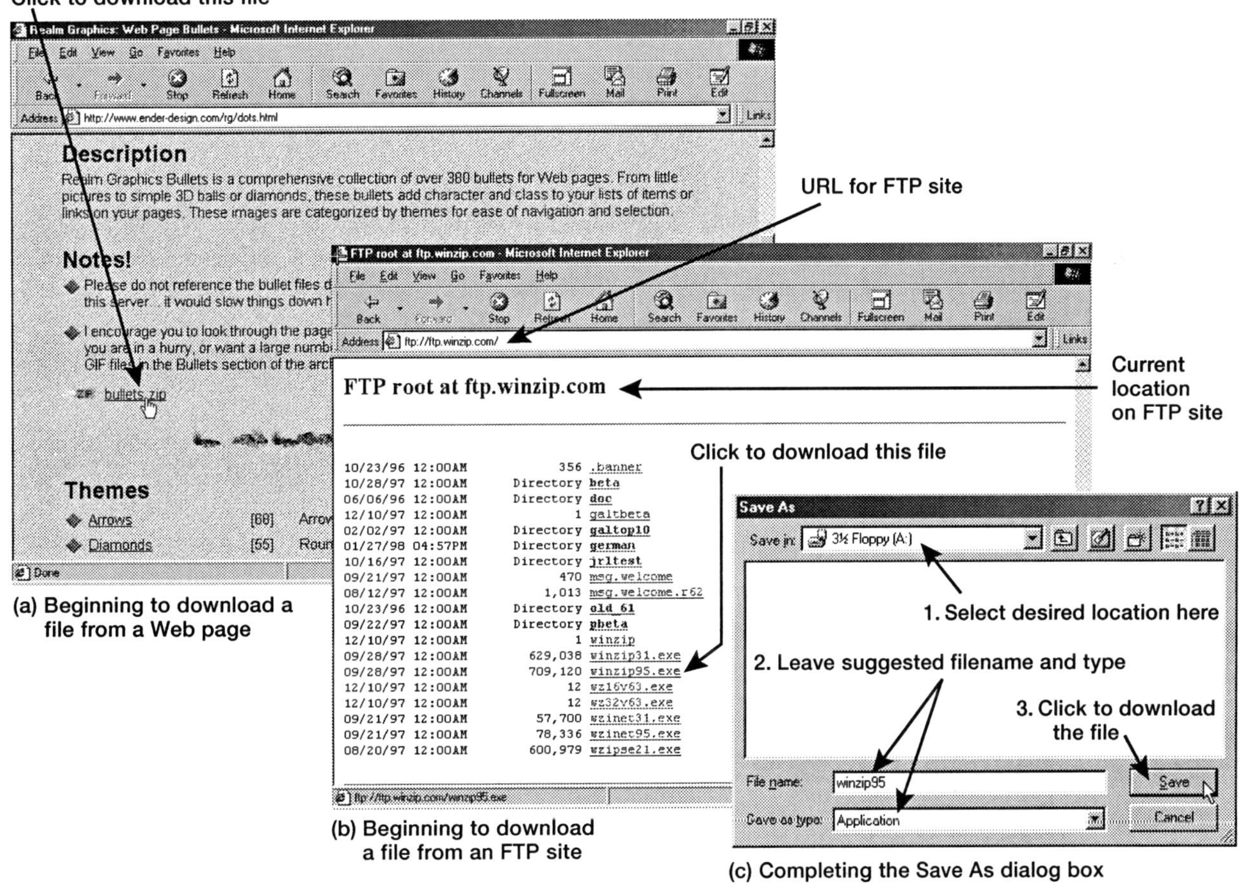

To avoid infecting your computer with a *computer virus* (a destructive software program hidden in a file) by downloading an infected file, be sure to use an antivirus software program regularly (search for "virus" using a search site for more information). Some antivirus programs can be set up to automatically check all files downloaded from the Internet before they are stored on your computer.

If you are working in a computer lab where more than one person uses the same computer, you may need to enter your user name, e-mail address, and mail server name in the Mail Preferences or Options screen before you can send or retrieve e-mail—ask your instructor for specific instructions for your network and browser.

Many e-mail programs include an *Attach* option that allows you to attach files to an e-mail message—this is often the easiest way to send a file to someone.

box shown in Figure NET 19c and then wait for the file to be downloaded; depending on the size of the file and the speed of your computer and Internet connection, downloading a file can take anywhere from a few seconds to several hours.

Many files downloaded from the Internet come **zipped** (compressed) for faster downloading and must be **unzipped** (decompressed) before you can use them; one zipped file may contain one or more files. Zipped files have the extension *.zip* and must be unzipped with a file compression program, such as *WinZip* or *Pkzip.* To unzip a file using a Windows-based file compression program (such as WinZip), open the file in My Computer or Windows Explorer—the appropriate file compression program should start automatically and then you can follow the instructions to unzip the file. To unzip a file using a DOS-based program (such as Pkzip), you will need to type the appropriate command using the Run dialog box.

Electronic Mail

Electronic mail (more commonly called **e-mail**) is the term used to describe sending electronic messages from one computer user to another over a network. E-mail can be sent and retrieved over the Internet using most Web browsers—the **Netscape Messenger** and the **Microsoft Outlook Express** programs can be accessed from within their respective browsers to send and receive electronic mail.

Sending Electronic Mail

It is common for Web pages to include e-mail hyperlinks that enable visitors to easily send an e-mail message to a particular person at that Web page's organization to ask questions, request information, and so forth. E-mail links are often addressed to the site's *webmaster*—the person in charge of the Web site—especially to send comments about the Web site. As shown in Figure NET 20a, to send an e-mail message using a hyperlink, just click on that hyperlink and complete the appropriate information.

To start a new e-mail in Netscape without using a hyperlink, click on the Mailbox icon or on the right edge of the status bar to open the Netscape Messenger Mailbox window (type your e-mail password, if requested), then click on the New Msg toolbar button, as shown in Figure NET 20b. (Internet Explorer users: Click on the Mail toolbar button and select *New Message,* as shown in Figure NET 20c.) Once the Message Composition or New Message window is displayed:

1. Type the e-mail address of the person you are writing in the *To:* box.
2. Type a short title of the message in the *Subject:* box.
3. Type the message itself in the message area (it is a good idea to make sure you leave a blank line or two after the message, since often the last few characters of a message are not transferred when the message is sent).
4. Click on the Send button to send the message.

If you send e-mail to the same person frequently, add their name, e-mail address, and a nickname to your mail program's *address book* by selecting *Address Book* from Netscape's Communicator menu or Outlook Express's Tools menu. Once a person is in your address book, you can type their address book nickname in the *To:* box instead of typing their complete e-mail address.

Receiving Electronic Mail

To check for new e-mail messages or to reread an old e-mail message using Netscape Navigator, click on the Mailbox icon , , or located

FIGURE NET 20
Sending an e-mail message.

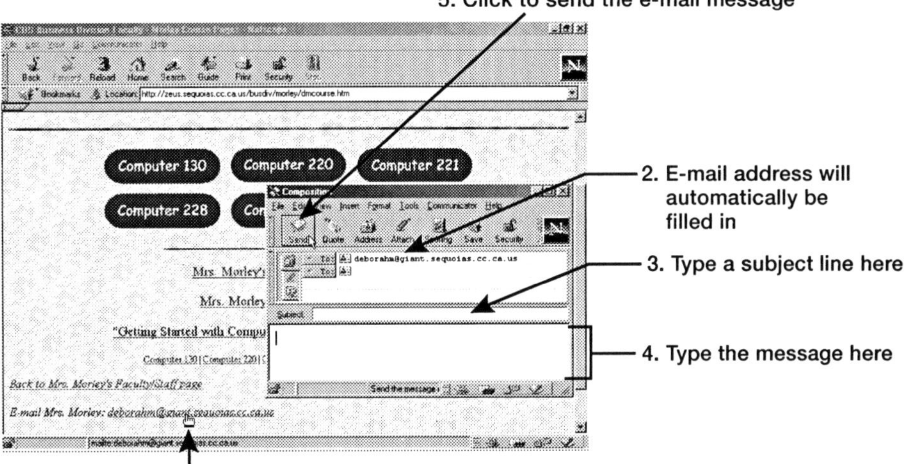

(a) Using an e-mail hyperlink

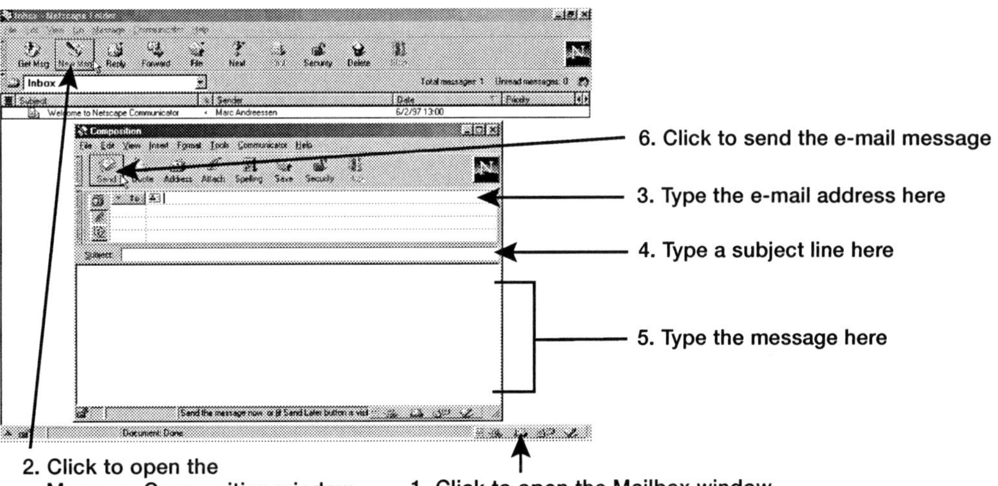

(b) Using Netscape Messenger

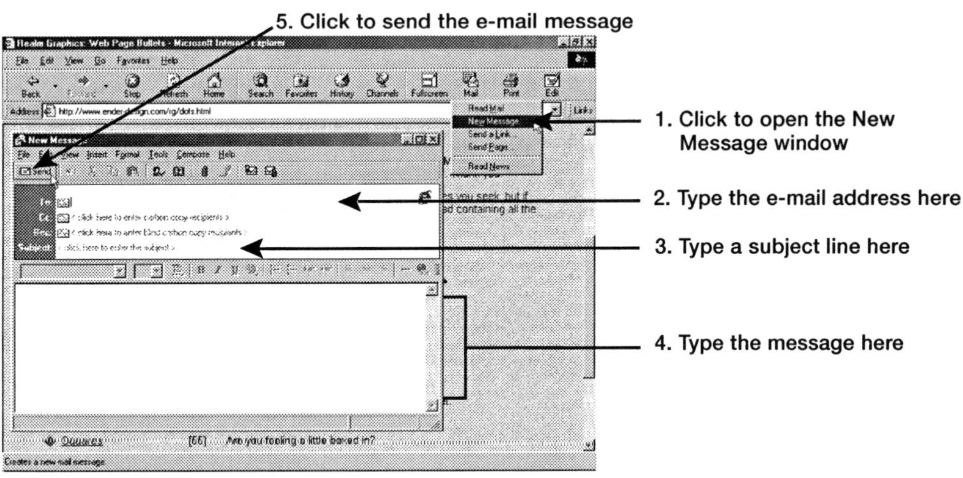

(c) Using Microsoft Outlook Express

FIGURE NET 21
Reading an e-mail message.

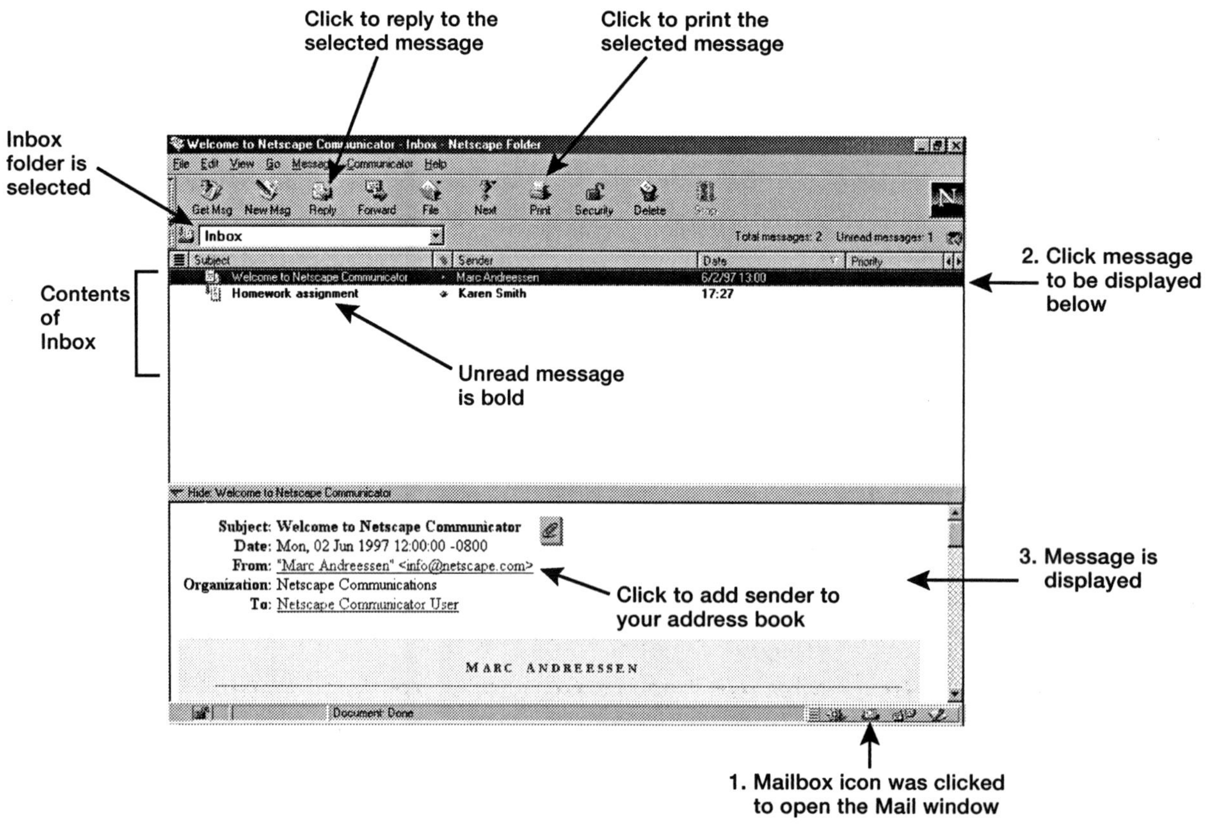

Netscape's Mailbox icon changes to reflect the status of your e-mail: before you have checked your mail, after you have checked your mail and still don't have any new mail, and when new e-mail has arrived. Netscape also places a small envelope icon on the Windows taskbar to indicate that you have new mail.

on the right edge of the status bar, as shown in Figure NET 21. (Internet Explorer users: Click on the Mail toolbar button and select *Read Mail* instead.) You will then usually be asked to type your password to ensure that only an authorized person is retrieving your mail; after typing it, your new e-mail messages will be retrieved to your Inbox folder. Clicking on a message will display it in the message area, as shown in Figure NET 21. To display an e-mail message in a new window instead of at the bottom of the screen, double-click on the message. E-mail messages remain in the Inbox folder until you delete them or file them into a different folder. To move a message to a different folder, right-click on the message and choose *File Message* (Netscape Messenger) or *Move To* (Outlook Express) from the message's shortcut menu (you can create new folders in either program using the mail program's File menu). You can also print a selected message using the Print toolbar button or start a reply message to the sender using the Reply button.

Creating a Web Page

Most Web pages are written in **Hypertext Markup Language (HTML),** which uses special codes called *HTML tags* embedded within the page's text to identify hyperlinks, formatted text, where graphical images should be displayed, and so forth. Basic Web pages are sometimes created in a text editor or word processor with the appropriate HTML tags typed in the appropriate locations, as shown in

FIGURE NET 22

A basic Web page and its corresponding HTML file.

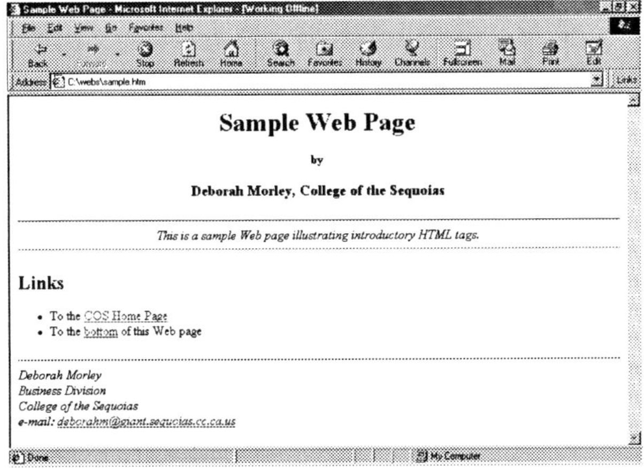

(a) The Web page displayed in Internet Explorer

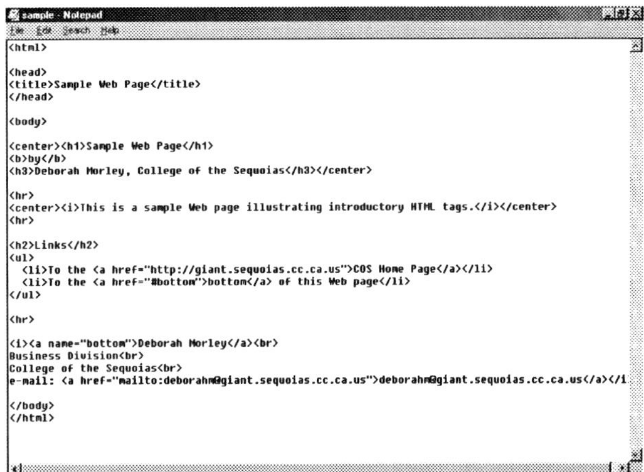

```
<html>

<head>
<title>Sample Web Page</title>
</head>

<body>

<center><h1>Sample Web Page</h1>
<b>by</b>
<h3>Deborah Morley, College of the Sequoias</h3></center>

<hr>
<center><i>This is a sample Web page illustrating introductory HTML tags.</i></center>
<hr>

<h2>Links</h2>
<ul>
  <li>To the <a href="http://giant.sequoias.cc.ca.us">COS Home Page</a></li>
  <li>To the <a href="#bottom">bottom</a> of this Web page</li>
</ul>

<hr>

<i><a name="bottom">Deborah Morley</a><br>
Business Division<br>
College of the Sequoias<br>
e-mail: <a href="mailto:deborahm@giant.sequoias.cc.ca.us">deborahm@giant.sequoias.cc.ca.us</a></i

</body>
</html>
```

(b) The Web page's HTML file displayed in Notepad—the HTML tags must be typed in the appropriate locations

FIGURE NET 23

Basic HTML tags.

Most HTML tags work in pairs; the <tag> marks the beginning of the text to be formatted and the </tag> marks the end of the text.

TAG	EXPLANATION
<title></title>	Marks the title of the Web page.
<center></center>	Centers the text.
<b></b>	Bolds the text.
<i></i>	Italicizes the text.
<h1></h1>,<h2></h2>, etc.	Marks headings (1 is the largest).
<ul></ul>	Marks an unordered list.
<li></li>	Marks each list item.
<a></a>	Marks a hyperlink (anchors the text to a link).
<hr>	Inserts a horizontal rule (a line across the screen).
 	Indicates a line break (starts a new line within the same paragraph).
<p>	Indicates a paragraph break (starts a new paragraph).

Web pages can also be created in some standard application software programs—such as Word, WordPerfect, PowerPoint, and PageMaker—and then converted from within those programs to HTML documents. Though creating Web pages in these programs often works adequately for simple Web pages and existing documents, the features available in these programs are much more limited than in Web publishing programs.

Figure NET 22. Many of the HTML tags used in the Web page in Figure NET 22 are explained in Figure NET 23.

More complex Web pages are usually created using special programs for creating Web pages (often called *HTML editors, Web publishing* programs, etc.), such as Netscape Composer, Microsoft FrontPage, Macromedia Dreamweaver, and so forth. Once the page has been created, it is saved as an HTML file using the *.htm* or *.html* file extension (depending on the Web server to be used) so it can be viewed using a Web browser and then is *published* (copied) to the appropriate Web server (usually belonging to a school, business, online service, or ISP); once a Web page is published, it can be accessed through the Internet.

SUMMARY

The Internet is the largest computer network in the world, consisting of a vast amount of data and files, as well as the World Wide Web—a collection of millions of Web pages. On the Internet, computers are identified by unique numeric IP addresses and text-based domain names, computer users are identified by e-mail addresses, and Web pages are identified by their Uniform Resource Locator or URL.

Web browsers are software programs that enable you to easily access the World Wide Web and other resources on the Internet; currently the two most widely used Web browsers are Netscape Navigator and Microsoft Internet Explorer. To move through the Web, hyperlinks are clicked and/or URLs are typed in the location/address field.

To help you find specific information on the Web, most Web browsers give you easy access to search sites. Web browsers also enable you to bookmark, save, and print Web pages; download files; and send and receive electronic mail.

KEY TERMS

Address field (NET 11)
Address toolbar (NET 11)
ARPANET (NET 2)
Bookmark (NET 12)
Client (NET 7)
Command toolbar (NET 9)
Commercial online service (NET 4)
Computer network (NET 2)
Directory (NET 15)
Domain name (NET 7)
Download (NET 19)
Electronic mail (NET 20)
E-mail (NET 20)
E-mail address (NET 8)
Favorite (NET 12)
File Transfer Protocol (NET 19)
FTP (NET 19)
Home page (NET 9)
Host (NET 4)
HTML (NET 22)
Hyperlink (NET 2)
Hypertext Markup Language (NET 22)
Internet (NET 2)
Internet address (NET 6)
Internet service provider (NET 4)
Intranet (NET 2)
IP address (NET 7)
ISP (NET 4)
LAN (NET 2)
Local area network (NET 2)
Location field (NET 11)
Location toolbar (NET 11)
Microsoft Internet Explorer (NET 3)
Microsoft Outlook Express (NET 20)
Modem (NET 3)
Netscape Messenger (NET 20)
Netscape Navigator (NET 3)
Search engine (NET 15)
Search site (NET 15)
Server (NET 7)
Status bar (NET 11)
Uniform Resource Locator (NET 8)
Unzipped (NET 20)
URL (NET 8)
WAN (NET 2)
Web browser (NET 2)
Web page (NET 2)
Web server (NET 7)
Web site (NET 9)
Wide area network (NET 2)
World Wide Web (NET 2)
Zipped (NET 20)

Quick Reference

NETSCAPE NAVIGATOR

TASK	INSTRUCTIONS
Check for new e-mail messages	Click on the Mailbox icon or or to open the Messenger program and check your mail.
Copy text from a Web page to another Windows application	Select (highlight) the appropriate text with the mouse and choose *Copy* from the Edit menu. Open the appropriate Windows application and select *Paste* from the Edit menu.
Create a bookmark for the current Web page	At the desired Web page, click on the Bookmarks button and select *Add Bookmark* (or choose *File Bookmark* to store the bookmark in an existing bookmark folder).
Download a file	Move to the appropriate Web page or type the URL address of the FTP site in the location field, then click on the appropriate hyperlink. Complete the Save As dialog box, then click *Save* to download the file.
Get help with the Navigator program	Select *Help Contents* from the Help menu.
Go to a bookmarked Web page	Click on the Bookmarks button and select the appropriate Web page.
Move through the pages visited in the current session	Click on the Back button to go backwards, click on the Forward button to go forwards, or select the desired page from the Go menu.
Move to a specific Web page	Click on its hyperlink or type its URL in the location field and press Enter.
Print a Web page	Click on the Print button (if the page is being displayed in frames, be sure that you are in the proper frame first).
Read an e-mail message	Click on the Mailbox icon or or to open the Messenger program, then click on the desired e-mail message.
Reload the current page	Click on the Reload button .
Save the text from a Web page to a file	Select *Save As* from the File menu (if the page is being displayed in frames, be sure that you are in the proper frame first). Type the desired filename, change the file type to either *Plain Text (*.txt)* to be opened with a text editor or word processor, or *HTML (*.htm)* to be opened with a Web browser, select the appropriate drive, and click *OK*.
Search for a Web page	Click on the Search toolbar button and select a search site. Type keywords and/or select appropriate directory categories until hyperlinks for appropriate Web pages appear; click on a hyperlink to go to that page.
Send an e-mail message	Click on the Mailbox icon or or to open the Messenger program, then click on the New Msg button. At the Message Composition window, type the appropriate e-mail address in the *To:* box, type a subject line in the *Subject:* box, type the message in the message area, then click on the Send button to send the e-mail message.

MICROSOFT INTERNET EXPLORER

TASK	INSTRUCTIONS
Check for new e-mail messages	Click on the Mail toolbar button and select *Read Mail.*
Copy text from a Web page to another Windows application	Select (highlight) the appropriate text with the mouse and choose *Copy* from the Edit menu. Open the appropriate Windows application and select *Paste* from the Edit menu.
Create a bookmark for the current Web page	At the desired Web page, select *Add to Favorites* from the Favorites menu.
Download a file	Move to the appropriate Web page or type the URL address of the FTP site in the address field, then click on the appropriate hyperlink. Complete the Save As dialog box, then click *Save* to download the file.
Get help with the Internet Explorer program	Select *Contents and Index* from the Help menu.
Go to a bookmarked Web page	Click on the Favorites button and select the appropriate Web page.
Move through the pages visited in the current session	Click on the Back button to go backwards, click on the Forward button to go forwards, or click the History toolbar button and select the desired page.
Move to a specific Web page	Click on its hyperlink or type its URL in the address field and press Enter.
Print a Web page	Select *Print* from the File menu or click on the Print button (if the page is being displayed in frames, be sure that you are in the proper frame first or select the option to print the frames as laid out on the page on the Print dialog box).
Read an e-mail message	Click on the Mail toolbar button and select *Read Mail,* then click on the desired e-mail message.
Reload the current page	Click on the Refresh button .
Save the text from a Web page to a file	Select *Save As* from the File menu (if the page is being displayed in frames, be sure that you are in the proper frame first). Type the desired filename, change the file type to either *Text File (*.txt)* to be opened with a text editor or word processor, or *HTML (*.htm)* to be opened with a Web browser, select the appropriate drive, and click *OK*.
Search for a Web page	Click on the Search toolbar button and type appropriate keywords or select appropriate categories until hyperlinks for appropriate Web pages appear; click on a hyperlink to go to that page.
Send an e-mail message	Click on the Mail toolbar button and select *New Message.* At the New Message window, type the appropriate e-mail address in the *To:* box, type a subject line in the *Subject:* box, type the message in the message area, then click on the Send button to send the e-mail message.

MODULE WCT

Using WebCT

AFTER READING THIS MODULE, YOU WILL:

1. Understand how to get started using WebCT
2. Understand WebCT course tools and their uses
3. Understand how to navigate your WebCT course
4. Understand how to communicate online with others in your class using WebCT
5. Understand how to take online quizzes and exams using WebCT
6. Understand how to check your progress in your WebCT course

Getting Started

Welcome to the world of online learning! You have this handbook because you are taking an online course in the WebCT environment. This handbook will answer some of your questions about WebCT, give some instructions on how to be an efficient online learner, and assist you in navigating your online course.

WebCT (World Wide Web Course Tools) allows both online instructors and online learners to tap into the power of the World Wide Web (the Web) in order to access information and to communicate with each other. Using WebCT, you will be able to

- Log on to your course
- Read online lectures
- Use course-specific e-mail
- Post to a course bulletin board
- Take online quizzes
- Access multimedia presentations over the Internet
- Communicate with guest content experts

Getting Started: Your Computer

Traveling a freeway requires a vehicle, and if your vehicle's engine is powerful and properly tuned, the better and faster your trip will be. Vehicle problems, however, slow you down. This may be a good reason why we see so many newer vehicles on the freeways!

Taking an online course can be similar to traveling down a highway, except now you are traveling the Information Superhighway, and your vehicle is your computer. The newer and more robust your computer, the faster and more efficient you will be as an online student. This means the more access power you have in your computer, modem, and Internet Service Provider (ISP), the better off you'll be. You will want to travel the Information Superhighway as efficiently as you can. You wouldn't want your vehicle to interfere with course navigation nor with course completion.

If you are comfortable with using your computer and the Internet, you may want to skip to the next section titled "Going to Class." If you are new to the world of technology or if you feel uncertain about technology jargon, it would be good to read this section to familiarize yourself with computer terms and concepts. These terms are significant both when you purchase a computer and when you use it.

Processor Speed Your computer has a speed that may be compared to the power in a pickup truck. Just as the engine horsepower determines the speed and power of your pickup, so the computer processor determines just how quickly the computer can process information. Older computers, like older engines, run more slowly. Just as engineers are getting more horsepower from newer engines, computer engineers are getting more power from newer processors. Computers identify the processor speed in megahertz (MHz). The higher the number, the greater the speed. If you have a slow computer but are interested in more processor speed, you can upgrade by purchasing a more powerful processor. However, be sure that all other hardware components will work in conjunction with the new processor.

Similarly, a slow modem or a slow ISP connection will make your computer seem slow when you are accessing information on the Internet. Your computer will access the Internet only as quickly as the slowest speed along your information access route. A minimum of 28.8Kbps modem speed and Internet connection is recommended.

Operating System (OS) OS refers to the type of computer operating-system software and how current that operating system is. You won't need to purchase a new computer in order to have a newer operating system. Many people simply purchase newer operating-system software over the Internet, from computer catalogs, or from a computer store. Operating systems, software packages, and Internet browsers use a numbering system that indicates product improvement with higher version numbers. WordPerfect 8 is an improvement over WordPerfect 7; Netscape 4 is an improvement over Netscape 3. Similarly, the OS number increases as newer OS versions are released. For example, Mac OS 8 is a Macintosh Operating System 8, which is newer than Mac OS 7 or 7.5. Windows 98 is newer than Windows 95.

Where can you find the type and version of your operating system? If you use a Macintosh, click on the Apple menu, drag to **About This Macintosh,** and release. A window will open showing the system-software information. Notice in Figure WCT 1 that *System Software 7.5.5* means this Macintosh is using OS 7.5.5.

If you use Windows, click the right-hand mouse button on **My Computer** on your desktop and look under **Properties** for your computer OS identification. Notice in Figure WCT 2 that *System: Microsoft Windows 95* means the OS is Windows 95. Windows 95 was improved and released as Windows 98.

A good rule of thumb is to use the current operating system, software, and browser. When a new version becomes available, you don't need it immediately, but you sure don't want to be two versions behind. If you don't keep up, it will be difficult to use the Internet on your computer. The ability to tell your employer that you took online courses will indicate that you have computer skills. The idea is to stay current.

FIGURE WCT 1
Macintosh Operating System

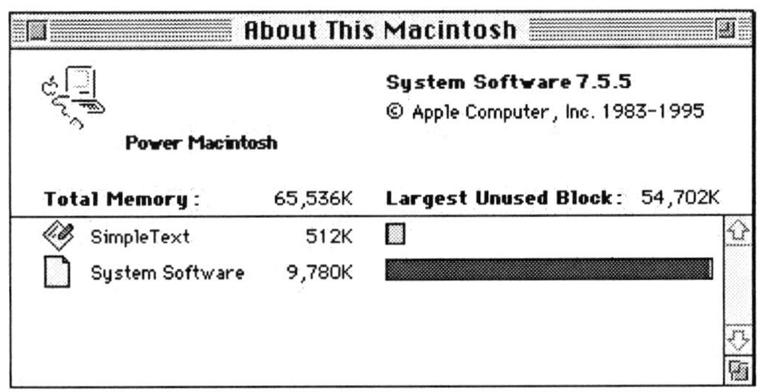

FIGURE WCT 2
Windows Operating System

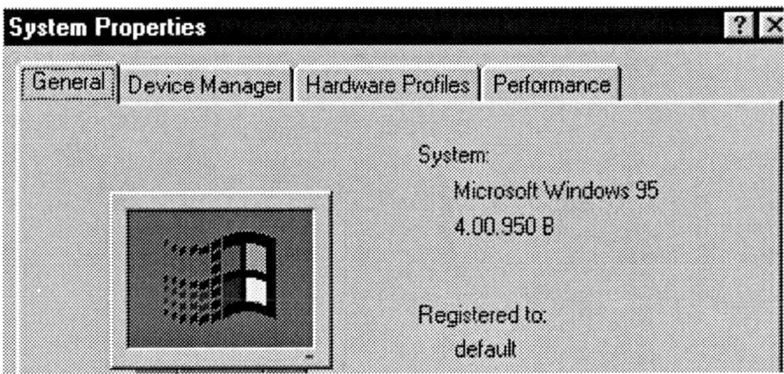

Your computer's OS will use a certain amount of computer memory for storage and operating. Before upgrading your OS, check to be sure your computer has enough memory to run the newer OS software.

Hard Disk Hard disk space, measured in megabytes or gigabytes, is the total amount of space your computer has for storage. It's easy to understand memory when you equate it with desk drawers and shelves. Your supplies and documents require space in the drawers and shelves just as your computer's OS, software, browser, and document files require hard drive space for storage. Software, browser and OS improvements offer more features — and that means these improvements require more memory for storage. In 1996, 750 megabytes of hard drive space sounded like an endless supply. In 1998, 6.5 gigabytes of hard drive space sounded like it might be sufficient for a lifetime. By early 1999 computers were being advertised that had 13.6 gigs of hard drive space. Just like automobile engineers improve automobiles, so computer engineers improve computers. So, hard drive space requirements expand as computer capabilities expand.

RAM Random Access Memory, or **RAM,** is the amount of memory your computer can access to run software, and can be compared to the amount of space on your desktop. If you have a small desktop, you won't have room for books, notebooks, pencils, notepads, and coffee cups on that desk! You will run out of space. The same is true of RAM. RAM allows software, documents, e-mail, browsers, and plug-ins to be open on your computer's desktop all at the same time. If your computer doesn't have sufficient RAM, you won't be able to have several items open at once.

In an online class, it is good to be able to have at least your browser and an integrated software package (word processor, spreadsheet, database) open at the same time. If you find you are short of RAM, you can purchase additional RAM for your computer. The price of RAM varies; sometimes it's cheap, sometimes more costly. The installation process isn't difficult, but if you don't feel confident, have a computer technician assist you.

Modem A modem connects your computer over your telephone line to your Internet Service Provider (ISP) which connects you to the Internet. Some modems are internal, some external; however, all modems have a speed at which they access and return data. You have probably heard "I have a 33.3 modem" or "I have 56K." This is modem-speed jargon! Get the fastest modem you can, which means the higher numbers. The more you access the Internet, the faster you will become, and thus, the more speed you will want. However, you should check the speed of your ISP because you may have a 56K modem, but your ISP may only serve the data at 33.3K. Data will be returned to you at the slowest speed on your route. Knowing your modem speed and the ISP modem speed will help you understand if you access data at a slower rate than you think appropriate. Remember that, over time, your ISP will keep improving its Internet connection speed, so even if you have a faster modem than ISP connection, your ISP will catch up. You will just be ahead of the game and won't need to purchase a newer modem.

External modems need to be configured or setup for the specific computer to which they are connected. If the configuration process is intimidating, seek assistance rather than wasting time.

Specifications The optimal computer specifications you should consider are

- 233 MHZ processor
- Windows 95 or PowerMac OS 8

- 2 GB hard disk drive
- 36 MG of RAM
- 28.8K modem, but consider buying 56K since it won't cost much more

Locating Your WebCT Class Once you have been given the URL or Web address of your WebCT class, type the address in the location bar of your Web browser and hit Return (Enter) on the keyboard (Figure WCT 3). If you have typed the address correctly, you will, barring any connection problems, arrive at your class. Online WebCT courses are password-protected. This password protects both the course and the student. No one can enter the course and access information about your progress and grade unless you share your login ID and password. Once you have a login ID and password, simply enter it on the appropriate lines (your login ID and password are case sensitive), and click on **OK** to enter the class (Figure WCT 4).

If you aren't assigned a login ID and password, then you will create your own account. At the bottom of the Welcome Page, you will see three choices as shown in Figure WCT 5. Once you click on **Create Account,** you will be asked for specific information including choosing a login ID and password. Be sure to remember your login ID and password for return entrance into the class.

Bookmarking the Web page for your online class will allow you to reach the site via the bookmark rather than typing in the URL every time you go to class.

You cannot change your login ID; however, if you were assigned an original password by your instructor, you would be well advised to change that password. Look on the course home page or an additional course tool page for the Password icon.

Click on this icon and follow the instructions. Be sure you remember the new password.

FIGURE WCT 3
Typing the URL for WebCT Course

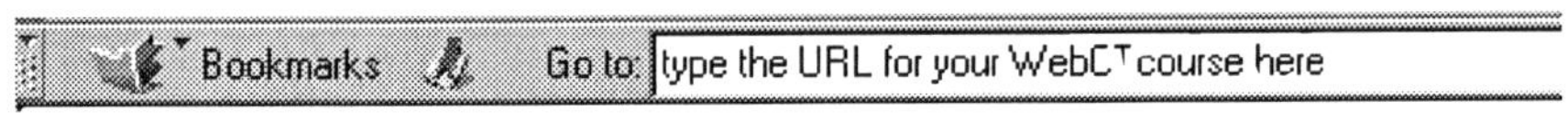

FIGURE WCT 4
Entering Username and Password

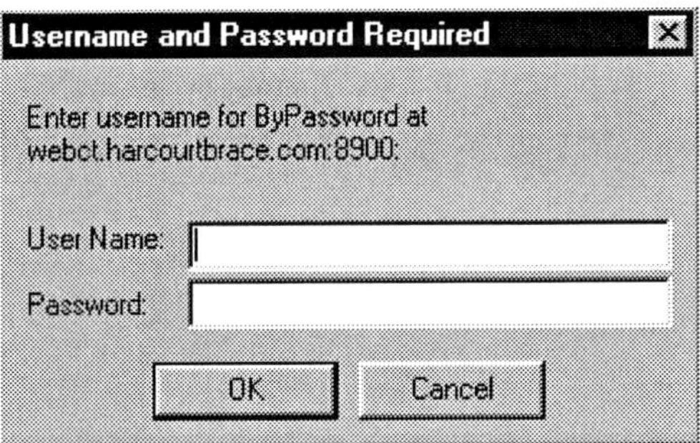

FIGURE WCT 5
Creating Your Own Account

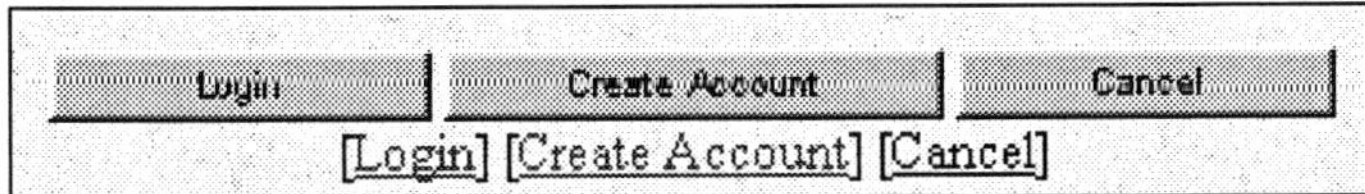

Getting Started: Your Web Browser

A Web browser is special software that allows users to explore and use the Internet. The two most widely used Web browsers are Netscape Communicator and Microsoft Internet Explorer. Keeping current with browser versions is important. If you aren't up-to-date, you may not be able to access some Web features.

WebCT supports both Netscape 3.0 and higher and Internet Explorer 4.0. Other Web browsers may not provide the functionality you will need for your WebCT online course. Therefore, one of these two Web browsers is your best choice.

What shall I do when I download software and am asked where to save it? Now that you are fully engaged in this online world, it is a good idea to make a download folder on your hard drive and then always download software and plug-ins from the Internet into this folder.

Downloading Software The two dominant Web browsers offer free download sites on the Internet.

Internet Explorer: http://www.microsoft.com/windows/ie/download/windows.htm

Netscape Communicator: http://home.netscape.com/computing/download/index.html

Visit the download site for the browser of your choice and follow the directions on that Web page. Download the full components of the browser. For example, with Netscape Communicator, download all files and save in the Download folder you will learn to create next.

To make a new download folder on a Macintosh

1. Open your hard drive.
2. Create a new folder by clicking **File** on the menu bar and dragging to **New Folder.**
3. Name the folder by typing **Download** over the highlighted words "untitled folder."
4. Download all software into this folder.

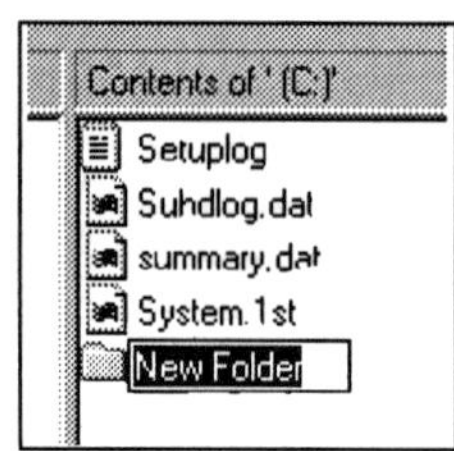

To make a new download folder on computers using Windows 95

1. Open **Explore Windows.**
2. Put your mouse on the **Contents of (C:)** (the right side of your screen).
3. Right-click and hold for **New ➤ Folder.**
4. Release and you will have a **New Folder** on your C drive.
5. Name the folder by typing **Download** over the highlighted words "New Folder."

When you click on a download link, you will get a dialog box asking where you want to save the file you're downloading and what you want to name it. The name in the **File Name** field isn't always intuitive, so feel free to rename the file. Name the file something that makes sense to you. Download it into the Download folder you created. Downloading can take several minutes depending on the size of the file. The download window will usually show the approximate time for the download to occur. If you realize you won't have the time necessary, you can always cancel the operation and try again later. If you create and maintain a Download folder, you will always know where downloaded files are stored and be able to easily access older download versions in order to delete them. If you don't delete them, they will use hard drive space.

Configuring Your Browser Configuring simply means adjusting the browser settings so they are compatible with your needs. You will need to enable Java and Java Script (Figure WCT 6a) in order to navigate your WebCT course.

You will also need to set the cache (in Internet Explorer, "Temporary Internet Files") to reload every time (Figure WCT 6b). This way you make sure that each time you visit a page in your WebCT course, your browser is showing you the latest version of the page.

Once you have your browser installed and configured so that Java is enabled, and cache is set to reload every time, you have the basic browser setup necessary for your online course. That is, unless your course requires plug-ins.

Plug-ins Your online instructor may have used multimedia features that will require an Internet plug-in. Plug-ins, such as RealPlayer, Quick Time, Shockwave Flash, etc., are similar to extras you install on your car's dashboard, such as a CD player. Browser plug-ins allow you to do such things as watch movies, listen to sounds, and play games on the Internet. Newer browser versions will often download and install basic plug-ins automatically as the browser downloads. In most instances, instructors will probably indicate that you need a specific plug-in and may even create a link to the download site for that plug-in. If the link is there, click on it and follow the instructions. Save the downloaded plug-in in your Download folder, then follow the installation instructions that came with it (usually found on the Web page from which you downloaded the plug-in or in a "Readme" file accompanying the downloaded plug-in). If you are not provided a link from which to download the plug-in, try visiting www.tucows.com. This site provides downloads of a wide variety of plug-ins.

Your computer should now be ready for your online course work. Go ahead and type the URL of your course in the browser location bar, bookmark the site, insert your login ID and password, and read that course home page. You are now officially an online WebCT student! Congratulations and good luck!

Bookmarks How and why do you bookmark a Web site? You bookmark on the Internet for the same reason you bookmark a book: to help you get back to the page easily! Internet users are efficient time managers when they bookmark Web sites they visit regularly.

FIGURE WCT 6

Configuring the Browser and Setting the Cache

(a)

Browser choices and appropriate directions to enable Java/JavaScript	
Netscape Navigator 3	Select "Options", "Network Preferences", then "Languages". Check both "Enable Java" and "Enable Javascript".
Netscape Navigator 4 (Communicator)	Select "Edit", then "Preferences". Under "Category", select "Advanced". Check both "Enable Java" and "Enable Javascript".
Internet Explorer 4	Select "View", "Internet Options...", then "Advanced". Find the section titled "Java VM" in the list. If it is not expanded, double-click on "Java VM". Check "Java logging enabled" and "Java JIT compiler enabled".

(b)

To set the cache	
Netscape Navigator 4 (Communicator)	Select "Edit", then "Preferences". Under "Category", expand "Advanced" by clicking on the '+', then select "Cache". In the section where it asks about comparing the cached document to the network document, check "Every time".
Internet Explorer 4	Select "View", "Internet Options...", then "General". In the section titled 'Temporary Internet Files', press the Settings button. Check "Every visit to the page".

To bookmark a site, you must be viewing that site. Once again, the steps differ a bit for a Macintosh and a PC. On a Macintosh in Netscape 4, click on the green bookmark in the menu bar and select **Add Bookmark** from the drop-down menu. On a PC choose **Bookmarks ➤ Add Bookmark.** The title of the Web page becomes the name of the bookmark. If the title doesn't mean anything to you, change the name of the bookmark on your Macintosh by accessing the Netscape icon on the menu bar ➤ **Bookmarks;** highlight (click on) the bookmark title and go to the menu bar to **Edit ➤ Get Info,** and then type the title you want over the highlighted words (Figure WCT 7).

To rename a bookmark on your PC, locate **Bookmark ➤ Edit Bookmark** and highlight the bookmark title (Figure WCT 8a); then, right click ➤ **Bookmark Properties ➤ Rename** and type over the highlighted words (Figure WCT 8b); press **OK.** If you bookmark several sites, group them into topically organized folders. *Note:* If you are using Internet Explorer, bookmarks are called **Favorites.**

Getting Started: Technical Troubleshooting Tips

You may have difficulty accessing your online course at various times. Your first inclination may be to call the instructor or the online help desk to report the

FIGURE WCT 7
Bookmarking on a Macintosh

FIGURE WCT 8
Bookmarking on a PC

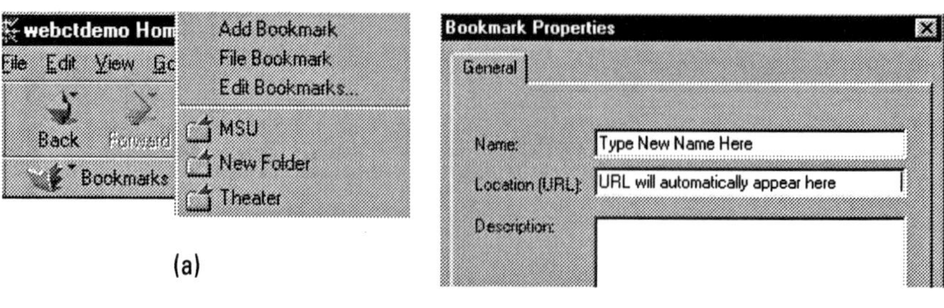

(a)

(b)

problem; however, you would be better off assessing the problem yourself first. Arming yourself with some technical troubleshooting tips will help you identify the problem or at least make you better able to discuss the problem with the online help desk.

WebCT resides entirely on a remote server computer. Only a few small components run on your own computer, and these components download and start running automatically. With a basic WebCT setup, there's nothing to install!

The Internet is a complex network that relies on working connections at all points on the route. As you use the Internet, the system itself routes you. Understanding the route complexities will help you troubleshoot and possibly help you isolate the problem. A good visual of the Web and your connection appears in Figure WCT 9 showing the various points where problems can occur.

Imagine yourself sitting at your computer. Your modem is plugged into your computer and into your telephone lines. This connects your computer to your ISP, which is connected via telephone lines to the Internet. World Wide Web sites are viewed using your browser. Web pages reside on various servers throughout the world. Already you can see many points on the route where problems can occur: your computer, your modem, your telephone connection to your ISP, your ISP, your ISP's connection to the Internet, your browser, the server that houses the Web pages you wish to view, not to mention the time variable involved. Internet traffic has rush hours just like the freeways. For this reason, it is important for you to develop some troubleshooting skills that will increase with practice and with assistance from others.

To troubleshoot, first check all cords and connections, restart the computer, and, if you still have trouble, follow the path of the connection and ask yourself these questions:

1. **Is the problem in my own computer?** For example, does your computer boot properly? Is this a monitor problem? If there seems to be a problem with your computer, troubleshoot the problem yourself, get a "techie" friend to help you, or hire a computer technician. If your computer seems okay, then move to the next level.

FIGURE WCT 9
The Internet System

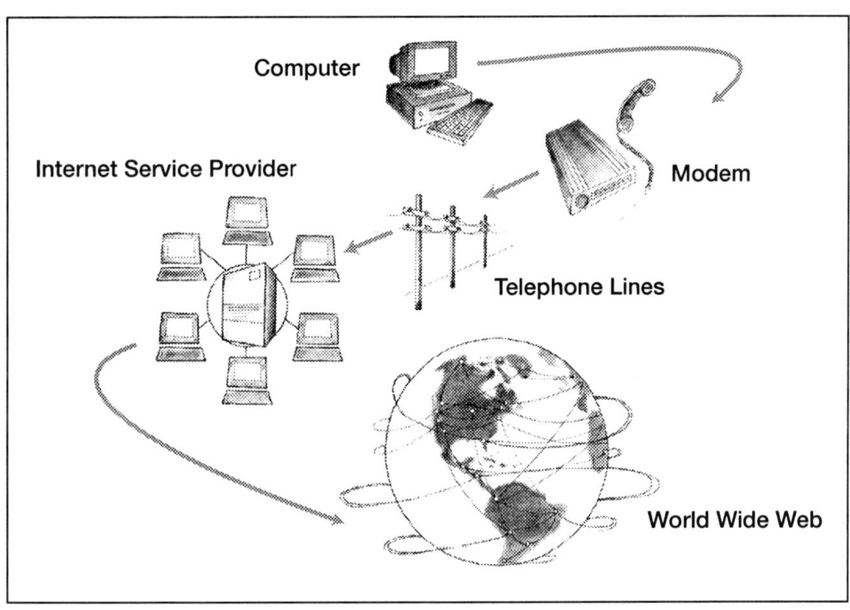

2. **Do you have your modem turned on?** Is the modem connection working? Have you configured your modem correctly? Modem configurations need to be accurate, and if you don't feel comfortable with this aspect, get help. Your ISP's technical help desk can usually help you here. If your modem connection is okay, move to the next level.
3. **Does the problem appear to be a phone line problem?** Sometimes this is difficult to detect. It may even be easiest to troubleshoot with your ISP before you contact the telephone company. If your ISP reports that everything is okay at their end, move to the next level.
4. **Are you attempting to access your online course from your work office?** If so, you may run into problems with your company's network security system. Your company may use firewalls to prevent random Internet access. You should clear your intentions with your company before using your office computer.
5. **Does this appear to be an Internet problem?** Here the possibilities are almost endless, and as the Web grows daily, these possibilities increase.

   a. You may have a DNS error. This message, as seen in Figure WCT 10, simply means that your browser cannot connect to the Web page you're trying to access. The Information Superhighway can't seem to get you to your destination. A couple of possibilities exist:

      - You misspelled the Web page address, or you clicked on a link whose author misspelled the Web address.
      - The Web page exists, but the connection between you and the page can't be made.

      As you can see from the image above, the problem was connecting with Yahoo — and it's unlikely that Yahoo's machines have gone down. The problem must have been elsewhere.

   b. You may receive an Error 404/File Not Found message indicating the Web page you want just isn't there. You may have misspelled the Web page address, or the page may have been removed or relocated and the link wasn't updated. Trying the address again is your only hope! It's similar to mail delivery: either the address is wrong or the people aren't there anymore.

What can I do if I get a DNS error? Check the Web page address to see if you typed it in correctly. If it's not misspelled, then it's a bad connection. Wait a few seconds and try again. This gives your ISP another chance to open the connection.

Getting Started: Successful Online Student Tips

As technology improves and as more and more people use the Internet, the number of online courses and learners increases. Those pioneer online learners and instructors report that taking an online course requires a special type of student.

FIGURE WCT 10
DNS Error

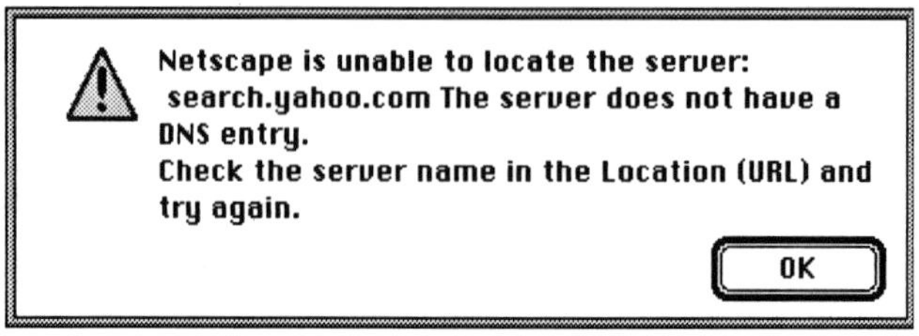

Netscape is unable to locate the server:
search.yahoo.com The server does not have a DNS entry.
Check the server name in the Location (URL) and try again.

OK

Because online students don't have to meet the same time and same place commitment that traditional students meet, these online students must be committed to the online course, have time management skills, and be able to work independently and usually in isolation. The face-to-face social element of the traditional classroom is missing. The items that follow may help you determine your success potential as an online student and may help you identify specific characteristics you should develop.

Successful online students

- Work independently and are self motivated. They don't need an instructor or boss to give them the next work assignment, a date for completion, and a peer group to work with. They don't need to be prodded to complete their work.
- Have time management skills. They know how much time needs to be allotted to all facets of their life:
  - Ask for clarification if information or instruction is unclear. These students don't waste time wondering. Successful online students recognize the online instructor as a facilitator of information and themselves as explorers and sharers of knowledge.
  - Have good keyboarding skills so they don't waste time and energy concentrating on the keyboard. Rather, they concentrate on course content and assignments.
  - Set aside a regular time for their online course. They recognize that this online course is not an "add-on" to their lives. This is not something they take care of when they have time. Knowing that an online course requires two to three hours each week for each hour of credit for the class, they participate regularly in the course. Successful online students log on and participate every day for thirty minutes to an hour rather than working once a week for five hours at a time. They establish offline student time similarly, and they meet that time commitment. Procrastination is the downfall of many online students.
- Have technology experience. They have worked with computers and the Internet so they aren't spending time learning the technology as much as they are learning course content. These students are not necessarily computer experts, but they do have computer experience.
- Participate actively in the online course. They interact with other students and the instructor in the online communication environments. These students don't monopolize the conversations in these environments, but they do more than "lurk" (sit on the sidelines and read but don't interact).
- Keep a calendar in view with course deadlines marked. If the instructor doesn't give deadlines, these students provide their own. Your online instructor may have designed the course so that you can put entries into your course calendar. Decide if you will use this calendar or a hard copy calendar of your own. Record your deadlines, when you posted assignments, when assignments are due, and tests are given. Regardless of which you chose, use it.
- Feel free to use hard copy of course pages to limit online time or to read offline when away from the computer. Online students are often nontraditional students who have times during the day when they are in the "waiting mode." They pick up their children after school, meet doctor appointments, go to laundromats, etc. Having hard copies of the online course in a folder they take with them or having their textbook with them makes it possible for them to work on their course during those times.

Work out a weekly schedule. Write half-hour slots for all waking hours down the side of the paper and the days of the week across the top. Fill in your committed times for jobs, meetings, family obligations, etc. Find open slots that can be dedicated to your online course for online time and for offline study time. Nothing short of an emergency should keep you from this online course time. If you are interrupted, remember to grab some catch-up time.

WebCT Course Management Tools provide information to your online instructor on the dates and times you access the course, how much time you spend on each page, and how many course tools such as glossary, goals, index, etc., you access. You can also find this information yourself under the My Progress icon. What you do as an online WebCT student is no secret to the instructor. Don't try to pull the wool over the online instructor's eyes!

WebCT gives you the option to Compile the Course Content, which means you can select specific course pages, compile them, and print them. Check the Compile feature via the Compile icon.

You may have additional characteristics which make you an efficient online student, and you may wish to develop some of those listed here. Just remember, the online course will move along without you if you lag behind!

Computer Monitor Tips

You can control the size of the font, the color combinations, the size of the viewing area on the screen, the size of the frames, and other items that affect your online world. To access these features, check your computer's **Control Panels** (for Macintosh) or **Properties** (for Windows). You can also control these items using your browser's **Preferences** or **Properties.**

> When you work in frames, which you do in WebCT (the button bar is in a frame, the lessons are in a frame, the bulletin board and private mail tools are in a frame), you must click inside the frame you wish to print.

Control the Viewing Area on Your Monitor If the content of a Web page is more than one screen, you will need to scroll down and across to read the entire Web page. You can do this by using the keyboard's down/up/across arrows or by using the scroll bars on the right and bottom of your screen. Be sure your screen is full size to your monitor by maximizing the screen: click on the box in the upper right corner of the screen, or click, hold, and drag the box on the lower right corner of your screen. If you are reading a Web page in a frame and wish to enlarge the viewing area of one frame, put the cursor over the frame border. When the arrow is precisely on the frame border, you should notice how the arrow changes. Click and drag the frame border to the size you desire. The frame will reload and will fill the wider viewing area.

> Resizing the viewing area or attempting any on-screen interactions while a page is loading may cause your computer to crash. This is especially important when loading audio or video files. Wait until the message on the bottom of your browser screen lets you know the document is finished loading.

Reliability and Documentation of Web Sites

Because publishing to the Web is not difficult, the amount of information added to the Web on a daily basis is phenomenal, and the result is that not all information on the Web is reliable. You will need to consider the reliability of Web sites when you do research. Ask yourself these questions:

1. Who is the author(s)?
2. What are the credentials of the author(s)? Are these credentials easily accessible? Do the authors introduce themselves? Are the authors part of a recognized educational institution or a reputable organization?
3. Is a link to the Web page creator provided so you can e-mail for verification?
4. Can you retrace the Web page to its home page? Does the page show when it was last updated?
5. Are the arguments that are presented logical? Are there links or references to other reputable sources?

These few questions will help you learn to assess Web-page reliability. You can also ask your librarian to provide an assessment. As you gain more experience, you will hone these critical-analysis skills.

Documenting or referencing a Web page is important in papers you write. When you cite an Internet source, you will need the following information:

- Author(s)
- Title of document
- Title of complete work (if applicable)
- Complete HTTP address (URL)
- Date you visited the site

Your online instructor will probably let you know which documentation style to use, but the most common are APA (American Psychological Association) or MLA (Modern Language Association). You can locate Web sites with information on these styles by conducting a Web search for "MLA" or "APA."

Going to Class

Course Home Page

The **course home page** is the gateway to your online course. It contains links to all the learning materials and is accessible from every other page in the course. On this course home page you will find:

- Information from your online instructor in the header and footer areas
- An icon that will link you to the course lessons
- Icons to additional "tool pages" that offer important course tools for you
- Icon links to a variety of pages your instructor wants you to be able to access

Let's look at a sample course home page in Figure WCT 11 to see what the icons do. Once you feel comfortable with the course home page, it is time to tackle those course lessons. And that's next!

FIGURE WCT 11
WebCT Home Page Icons

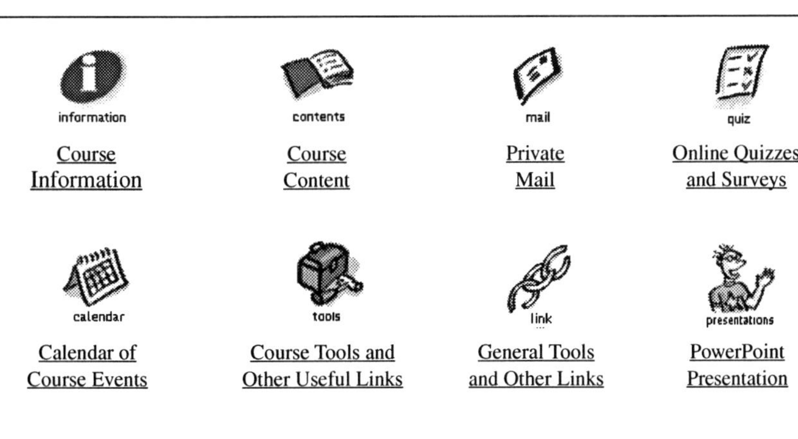

Course Information links to information provided by your instructor about your course, such as the syllabus and specifics about course expectations.

Course Content links to the course lessons and instructor lectures — the actual course content.

Private Mail links to your private e-mail box within WebCT.

Online Quizzes and Surveys links to class quizzes and tests.

Calendar of Course Events contains important course dates. Be sure to check here regularly!

Course Tools and Other Useful Links provides additional links to such items as how to create a customized study guide and how to access a course glossary, chat room, course search tools, and to resume the lessons where you left off.

General Tools and Other Links provides links to your grades, to your progress, to change your password, to student presentations and home pages.

PowerPoint Presentation links to a student presentation tool that lets you place documents into the course for others to view.

Familiarizing yourself with the course home page before you actually begin the course will help you navigate the course more smoothly! Go ahead and click on the icons on your online course home page to see where they take you. Read the headers and footers your instructor places on this course home page. These headers and footers are easily changed by your instructor and contain important information for you.

Why do some courses link to a Table of Contents and some don't? Making a Table of Contents available is the instructor's choice. If the link to the lessons takes you directly to the lessons and bypasses the Table of Contents, that's simply the way your instructor chose to design the course.

Your Course Lessons

Button Bar

Many of your WebCT lessons will have a button bar either on the top or the left side of the lesson page. This button bar contains icons put there by your instructor and may change from lesson to lesson and course to course, but knowing what these icons do will help you use them to your advantage. (A sample lesson button bar appears at the left.)

Navigational Tools

The group of six small buttons shown in Figure WCT 12 are navigational tools and help you navigate or move through the course.

Why do some of the button bar icons in Figure WCT 13 have little arrows below the image? Those arrows were purposely placed there by your instructor because they contain important information for that specific lesson. It's always a good idea to click on those icons to view that information.

Glossary

Glossary is just like the glossary you would normally find at the end of a textbook, except here it is online. Much of what we understand about a subject is directly related to content vocabulary, which is why your instructor chose to put words and definitions in the online course. It only makes sense then for you to access those definitions and learn the words. You can do that in three ways.

When working in your WebCT course, *always use your WebCT navigational tools* rather than your browser tools. For example, use **Pg Back** rather than the **Back** button on the browser, use **Pg Fwd** rather than the **Forward** button on your browser, and use the **Home** button rather than the **Home** button on your browser. The browser buttons move you through your Internet path and may just move you right out of your course. The WebCT navigational tools move you back and forth through the course lessons. The WebCT navigation tools are your better choice here.

FIGURE WCT 12
WebCT Navigational Tools

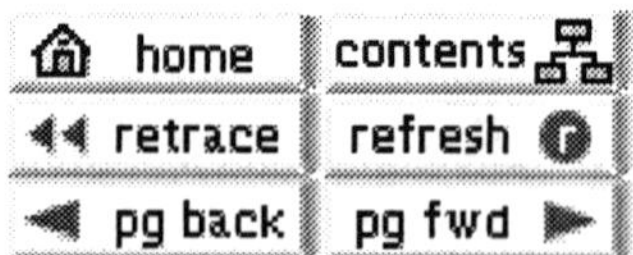

Home returns to the course home page.
Contents returns to the Table of Contents.
Retrace allows you to retrace your steps. If you have followed a hyperlink, retrace will take you back to your place in the course.
Refresh will reload the current page of content. For example, if **Targets** are viewed, clicking on refresh will return the current page of content.
Pg back takes you back one page in the lessons as defined by the order in the Table of Contents.
Pg fwd takes you forward one page sequentially in the lessons.

The one browser button that may come in handy is **Reload.** If you receive a "Transfer Interrupted" message or need to load the lesson again, use the browser **Reload** button.

FIGURE WCT 13
WebCT Course Content Icons

FIGURE WCT 14
Navigating the Glossary

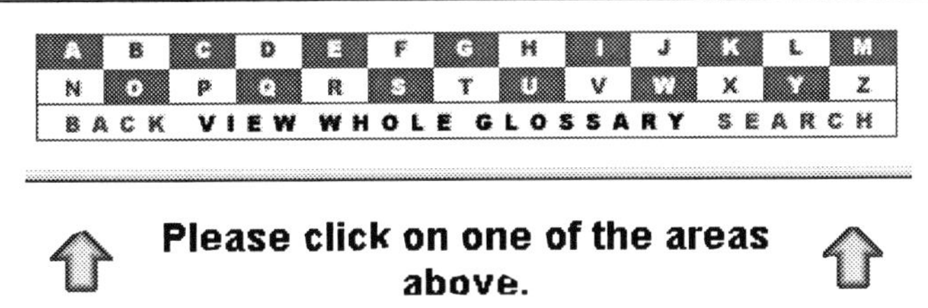

- Click on the **Glossary** icon on the button bar to reveal the image shown in Figure WCT 14 above. Here you can click on the words **View Whole Glossary** and do just that — view the whole glossary.
- Notice that the words are alphabetical so you can view one letter at a time.
- You will notice in your lesson text (Figure WCT 15 below) that some words are underlined. This means they are linked to the Glossary, and if you click on the word, a pop-up window (Figure WCT 16) will show you the definition. Just click on the **Close** button to return to the lesson.

FIGURE WCT 15
Hyperlinked Glossary Terms

- You started out on a hike from camp. You took a compas and kept track of each leg of your hike (distance and direction). You now want to return to camp. In which direction and how far away is camp?
- I am flying in a plane that can travel at 150 mph (with respect to the air). There is a southwest wind of 80 mph. In which direction should I travel to head directly north, and what will my resultant velocity be, with respect to the ground?

FIGURE WCT 16
Glossary Pop-Up Window

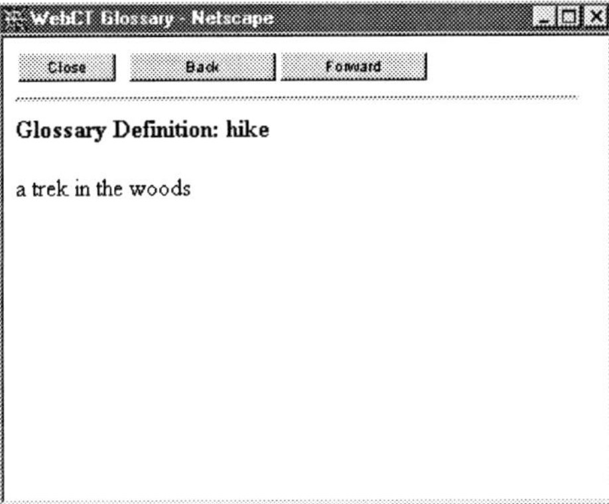

Search

The **Search** tool functions like an Internet search engine except that the WebCT search tool searches only the course material, not the entire Internet. The search tool opens a window with two frames: a query frame and a results frame.

Query frame In the query frame (Figure WCT 17a), you choose how to search the site: by Index, Title, Heading, or All Text. Enter your search term in the text box. The results including links to all the pages containing the search term will appear in the results frame.

Results frame See Figure WCT 17b below.

Index

The **Index** tool links to the course index, which links all the entries in the course to the content page where the entry can be found. If the instructor hasn't indexed any entries, then the index page will be blank.

References

The **References** tool links to bibliographic sources called Resources. A resource may be a book, an article, or hyperlinked Internet address (URL) that is relevant to the lesson. The arrow below the icon indicates that the instructor purposely inserted references on the lesson, so it is a good idea to click on the **References** icon to access those resources.

Targets or Goals

Both instructors and students need to know the goals or objectives of any lesson. WebCT usually calls these targets. Haven't you ever asked yourself, "Why are we doing this?" The answer can be found under the **Targets** icon. The instructor shares the lesson goals in the special targets area. Notice the small arrow under the icon? Remember, this means your instructor chose goals for the lesson. It's a good idea to click on the icon and check out those lesson goals. Chances are the course tests relate to the course goals!

FIGURE WCT 17
WebCT's Search Tool Query Frame and Results Frame

(a)

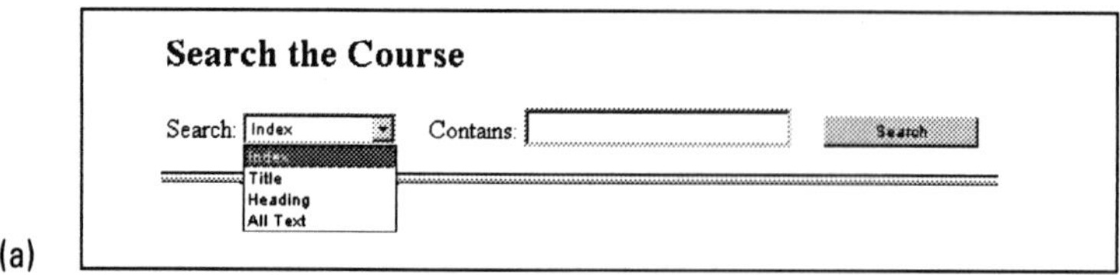

(b)

Search the Course

Search: All Text Contains: vector Search

Search Results

Keyword: vector, Search Selection: Title
What is a Vector?
What Can a Vector Do for Me?
Vector Review
How do we Describe Vectors?
Describing Vectors in Terms of Their Components
Vector Length
Vector Angle

FIGURE WCT 18
My Notes Text Box

Notes What Can a Vector Do for Me?

Edit	Delete	View All	Page List	Done

There are no notes for this page

Edit lets you add notes or edit notes.
Delete lets you delete notes.
View All shows all notes for the appropriate lesson titles.
Page List lists all the pages in the online course and links the lessons to your notes for that lesson. This is a nice feature since you can link to a particular lesson and study from your own notes.

My Notes

Just as the words suggest, **My Notes** allows you to take notes in each lesson — in other words, you don't need your own paper and pencil because you can take notes right on your computer. Click on **My Notes** and a text box opens to allow you to take notes. The notes for each lesson are automatically labeled with that lesson's title. No one but you can view your lesson notes because they reside inside your special course area. Clicking on **My Notes** gives you the choices shown in Figure WCT 18.

Self Test

The **Self Test** icon allows you to check your knowledge on the lesson content. These self-tests are inserted into the course just for your personal benefit (Figure WCT 19). You click on the answer you believe is correct and then get immediate feedback as shown in the figure. No

FIGURE WCT 19
Self Test

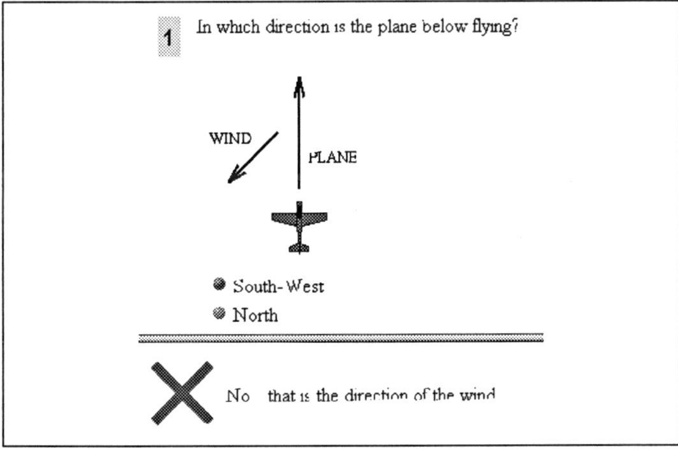

score is recorded; no record remains. It's just for your eyes. These self-tests are all multiple-choice questions.

General Course Tools

Change Your Password

password

Once you are logged into your WebCT course, your instructor may allow you to change your own password. Should you change that password? That's up to you, but you certainly may if your instructor makes available the **Password** link. Your login ID will remain the same, but if you change your password, be sure you remember the new one.

Resume Session

resume session

Resume Session functions like a bookmark in a regular textbook. When you stop working on a lesson, you bookmark the page so you know where to resume. How do you do this in a WebCT course? You simply click on the **Resume Session** icon, and you will automatically be linked to the lesson you had been viewing when you logged off.

Compile Lessons

compile

Perhaps you want to work in your WebCT course but need to be away from your computer. The **Compile** icon will link you to the lesson titles. You select the lessons you want compiled by clicking on the check box before each title. Then click on **Continue,** and the text of the selected lessons will appear. You can print them now and then read them later at your convenience.

Communicating in Class

Online discussion is thinking together and sharing ideas. Discussions require regular involvement on everyone's part. If your class uses bulletin board discussions, log in to your class regularly to participate. Logging into your course infrequently will limit participation. Watch for the *New Mail* and *New Bulletins* icons on the course home page or other tool pages. These indicate new messages have been received since the last time you logged into the course.

Once you've sent an e-mail or posted a message in the bulletin board, you can't take it back, so participate thoughtfully!

Traditional classroom learning relies on more than reading a text and attending lectures. Learning also takes place during discussion on course content, not only publicly during class but also privately from instructor to student and student to student. Discussions build and nurture learning communities, and generally in these discussions we experience the richness of learning. Discussion in an online course is at least as important as a traditional classroom, because the online class isn't in a face-to-face situation. Therefore, your online class discussions are an important component of your course.

Online discussions are referred to as either synchronous or asynchronous. Knowing where these words come from helps us understand their meaning: *a* means *without* or *not, syn* means *together,* and *chron* means *time. Asynchronous* then means "not together time" or "not together at the same time." *Synchronous* means "together time" or "communicating at the same time," also called "real time." Two WebCT communication environments are asynchronous: **e-mail** and **bulletin boards.** Two communication environments, **chat** and **whiteboard,** depend upon participants being in the environment at the same time.

WebCT provides communication environments that are both private and public. Here you have the opportunity to interact with others, to develop ideas, to pose questions. In other words, it is important to do more than just post your own ideas. It is also important to read and respond to the postings of others. The creation of an online learning community will make your online course more than just an online version of a correspondence course where you don't get to interact with others.

In order to understand these communication environments, relate them to "real world" communication. If you sent a personal letter to someone, it would be private. If you put a notice on a bulletin board, it would be public, and readers could respond on the bulletin board itself, or they could contact you personally. Chats take place between two or more people at the same time. Sometimes people actively participate in the conversation, and sometimes they listen (or lurk). These same concepts apply to the online environment. Mail is private and can only be viewed by the recipient; bulletin boards are public; chat is public with talkers and listeners.

Private Mail (asynchronous)

Your online course includes e-mail as a private communication environment within your WebCT course. The WebCT mail system provides three main functions: the ability to send, read, and search for mail messages.

Notice the two mail icons. Both give access to the mail room. The **Mail** icon may be located on the course home page, on an additional course tool page, and on the lesson button bar. The **New Mail** icon with radiating lines around it alerts you to new messages, but it will never appear on a lesson's button bar.

When you click on the **Mail** icon, you arrive at your private mailbox (Figure WCT 20). The mailbox features folders into which you can organize messages in ways that work for you. When you open your mailbox, you'll see it's arranged into three frames: left, top, bottom. The left frame provides the mail options, the top frame shows the list of messages that have been posted, and the bottom frame shows the messages and your options for acting on the message.

Now, let's look at each frame separately.

Understanding the Top Frame

The top line tells which folder is being viewed (see "Understanding the Left Frame" for explanation of **Folder**) and which of the folders messages are being viewed.

FIGURE WCT 20
Mailbox

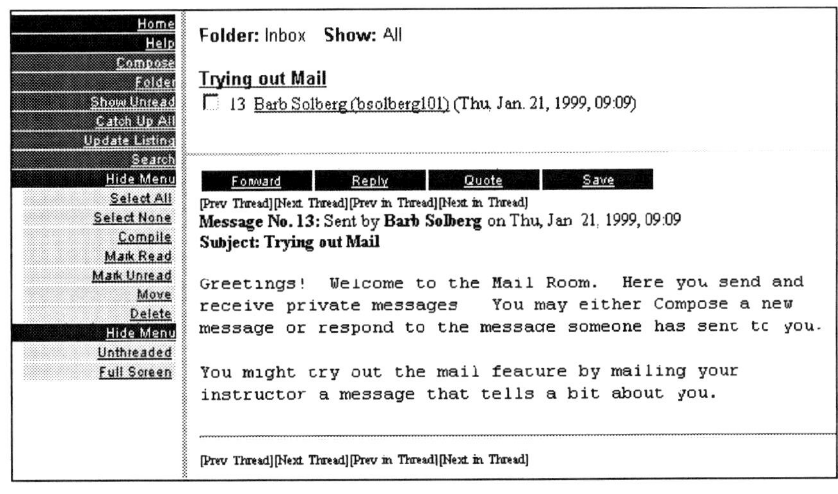

What is the purpose of the box next to the message number? This box allows users to select individual messages or to choose Select All to move messages into folders, delete, or compile them. You select messages individually by clicking in the box or, as a whole, by clicking on Select All in the left frame. Try it! Clicking in the box again will remove the check.

FIGURE WCT 21
Top Frame of the Mailbox

Folder: Inbox **Show:** Unread
Trying out Mail
☐ 13 Barb Solberg (bsolberg101) (Thu, Jan 21, 1999, 09:09) NEW

The next line shows "Trying Out Mail" is the subject, with message #13 listed (Figure WCT 21).

NEW at the right of a message indicates that this message has not yet been viewed. In this instance, the **New Mail** icon would be visible on the home page.

Notice all the links in Figure WCT 21. Everything that is underlined is linked for your viewing. To read the "Trying out Mail" thread, click on those words. To read one of the individual messages, click on the linked words next to the message number. The bottom frame shows the message.

Understanding the Bottom Frame

The top blue line of the bottom frame of the mailbox offers four choices as shown in Figure WCT 22 below.

When you view mail in the Full Screen mode, you will notice a **Listing** option (Figure WCT 23a). Clicking on **Listing** will display the message listing in the right frame. You will be able to view all messages.

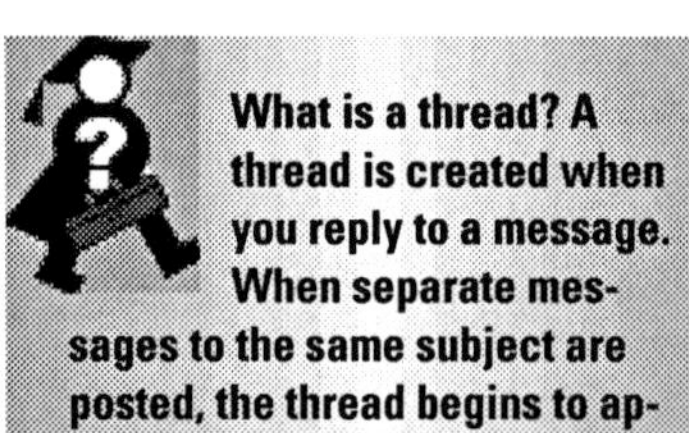

What is a thread? A thread is created when you reply to a message. When separate messages to the same subject are posted, the thread begins to appear in chronological order.

The next line contains the words shown in Figure WCT 23b. Notice that these same choices appear at the bottom of the message. When these are linked, they provide navigation through the messages. **Prev Thread** or **Next Thread** moves between threads. **Prev in Thread** or **Next in Thread** moves inside the thread.

The next line in the bottom frame lists the message number, sender, date, and time (Figure WCT 23c). Sometimes you will see [Branch from no _] because the message is a reply to another message and that message is linked for easy access. Also included is the subject title. A subject title preceded with an *re.:* indicates a reply to a previous message.

Next is the message itself (Figure WCT 23d).

FIGURE WCT 22
Bottom Frame of the Mailbox

Forward	Reply	Quote	Save

Forward allows you to send the message to another person.

Reply allows you to reply privately to the person who sent the message.

Quote allows you to include the message in your reply. Here you can put your cursor inside the message text and respond to specific points. Because you are in private mail, the message will return to the original sender.

Save allows you to save the message to your computer or to a disk. A window will open asking you to name the file and specify where the message should be saved. You should consider naming the saved file something descriptive so you will remember what the message is about.

FIGURE WCT 23
Bottom Frame of the Mailbox

(a)

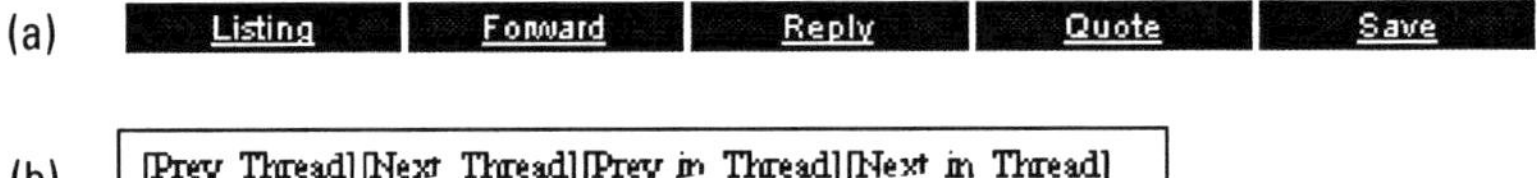

(b)

(c)

Message No. 13: Sent by **Barb Solberg** on Thu, Jan. 21, 1999, 09 09
Subject: Trying out Mail

(d)

Greetings! Welcome to the Mail Room. Here you send and receive private messages You may either Compose a new message or respond to the message someone has sent to you.

You might try out the mail feature by mailing your instructor a message that tells a bit about you

Understanding the Left Frame

The left frame provides a variety of choices to make you an efficient mail user. Notice that one image (Figure WCT 24a) shows more mail features than the other (Figure WCT 24b). If you click on **Message Menu. . .** and **Options Menu. . .** (the choices in red lines), you'll see a drop-down menu of additional features. Let's look at these features:

- **Home** links to the course home page.
- **Help** reveals a help menu to assist in mail use. This is worth a visit!
- **Compose** reveals a window in which you compose your message. Use this to begin a new thread but not to reply to a message (see "Understanding How to Compose A Message" below).
- **Folder** reveals a screen that allows you to create, sort into, and read individual mail folders (see "Understanding Folders" below).

FIGURE WCT 24
Left Frame of the Mailbox

(a)

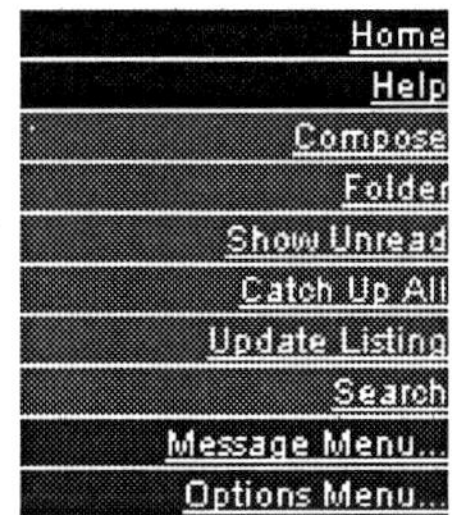

(b)

Home
Help
Compose
Folder
Show Unread
Catch Up All
Update Listing
Search
Hide Menu
Select All
Select None
Compile
Mark Read
Mark Unread
Move
Delete
Hide Menu
Unthreaded
Full Screen

- **Show All** will show all messages, not just unread messages. If you click on *Show All,* it will toggle with *Show Unread* which shows only unread messages.
- **Catch Up All** will mark all messages as read.
- **Update Listing** functions like Reload on your browser buttons — it will update the list of unread messages.
- **Search** provides the opportunity for more advanced searching in the mail box. A search screen will appear in which you select specific information for your search (see "Understanding Search" below).
- **Message Menu** reveals the following seven features:
  1. **Select All** will put a check mark in the selection box before each message so that you can deal with all messages at once.
  2. **Select None** removes the checkmark in the box before each message.
  3. **Compile** provides the opportunity to select, compile, and display all selected messages in the bottom frame for viewing, printing, and/or saving.
  4. **Mark Read** marks all or selected messages as read.
  5. **Mark Unread** marks all or selected messages as unread.
  6. **Move** gives you the ability to move a selected message into a specific folder.
  7. **Delete** provides the ability to delete a selected message.
- **Options Menu** reveals the last two options:
  1. **Unthreaded** shows the messages aligned left and in chronological order.
  2. **Unthreaded** toggles with **Threaded,** which shows messages in their threaded order.
     - **Unthreaded** Notice the left alignment and chronological order (Figure WCT 25a).
     - **Threaded** Notice the indented feature shows original post and responses to that thread (Figure WCT 25b).
- **Full Screen** opens one large frame on the right. This is handy if you are reading longer posts. **Full Screen** toggles with **Split Screen,** which divides the screen horizontally into top and bottom frames.

FIGURE WCT 25
Threaded and Unthreaded Options

(a)

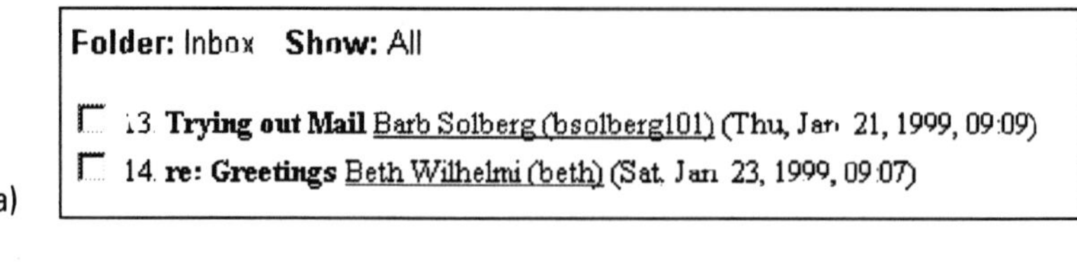

(b)

re: Greetings
9. -> Beth Wilhelmi (beth) (Wed, Jan. 20, 1999, 10:52) NEW
14. Beth Wilhelmi (beth) (Sat, Jan. 23, 1999, 09:07)
11. -> Beth Wilhelmi (beth) (Wed, Jan. 20, 1999, 11:01) NEW

FIGURE WCT 26
Compose a Message

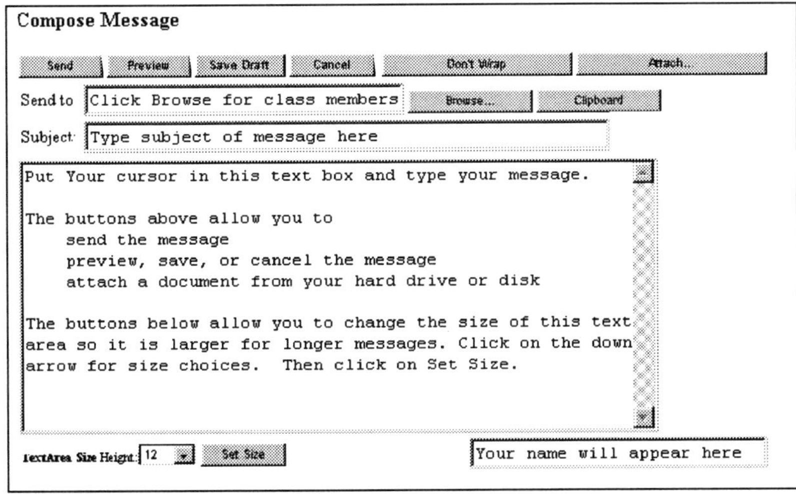

Understand How To Compose and Send a Message

You send a message one of three ways:

1. Begin a new thread
2. Reply to an existing message
3. Forward a message

Begin a New Thread To send a new message with a new subject line, click on the **Compose** button in the left frame to reveal the Compose Message window (Figure WCT 26). The **image** indicates what to do in **Compose.** To send a message to more than one recipient, hold your shift key as you click on the names. These names will automatically be inserted into the *Send to:* area and will be separated by commas. Click the **Send** button to send the message.

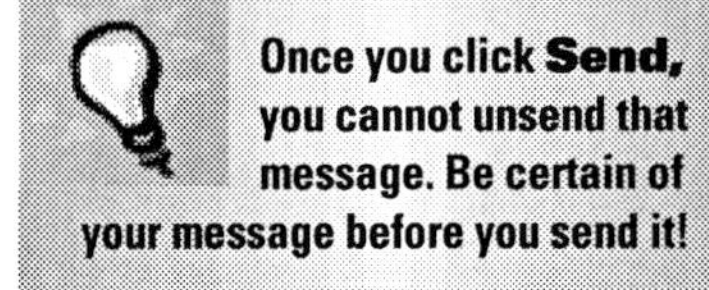

Reply to an Existing Message **Reply** allows users to answer a message. Clicking on **Reply** (Figure WCT 27a) when viewing a message will provide a blank text box for your reply. Notice the subject is automatically inserted in the **Compose Message** subject box (Figure WCT 27b). This is because you are replying to that subject thread. Remember to put your cursor in the text box before you begin typing your message The **Quote** option is helpful when you want to address particular points in a message. **Quote** allows you to insert your cursor inside lines of the original message and respond to specific parts of the message. Click on **Send** to send your reply.

Forwarding a Message If you read a message and want to forward it to someone else, use the **Forward** option (Figure WCT 27a). As in **Quote, Forward** provides a text box containing the message to be forwarded. You will be asked to specify the recipient of the message through the **Browse** feature.

Understanding Folders

Folders allow you to sort your mail. Each user has the folder choices as shown in Figure WCT 28.

FIGURE WCT 27
Reply to a Message

(a)

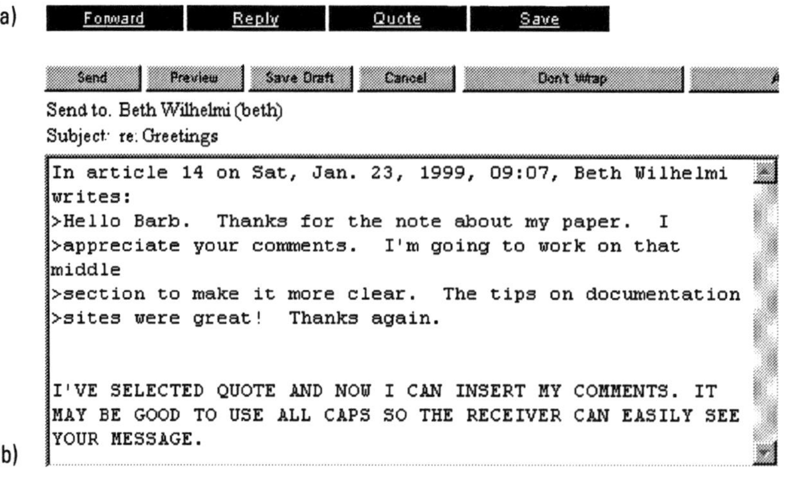

(b)

What if I start a message and want to finish it later? Use **Save Draft** at the top of the mail editor. To send a draft e-mail later, from the left frame choose **Folder** and then the Draft folder. A list of draft messages will appear. Click on the message to display the content. The **Compose Message** window will appear with the message. Complete the message, press **Send,** and WebCT will immediately send the message and move it from the Draft folder to the Outbox folder.

FIGURE WCT 28
Folder Choices

New Folder | Folders... | Cancel

Folder	Unread	Total
All	5	9
Draft	0	0
Inbox	0	2
Outbox	5	7

All contains all messages.
Draft contains unsent messages that have been saved as drafts.
Inbox contains all received messages.
Outbox contains all sent messages.

To create new folders, click on the **New Folder** button to display the "Folder Addition" window (Figure WCT 29). Type a new folder name in the text box and click on **Continue.** The new folder will be added to the list. You can create folders that will allow you to organize messages in ways that are helpful for you. For example, you might want to consider creating a special folder for messages from your instructor.

FIGURE WCT 29
New Folder

Folder Addition

Name:

Continue | Cancel

FIGURE WCT 30
Searching Folders

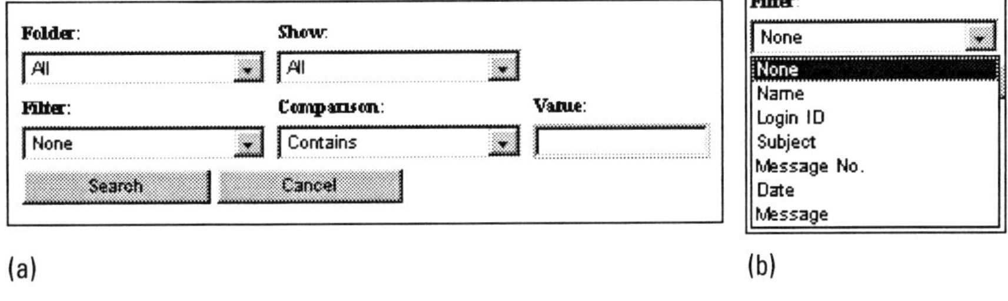

(a)

Filter:
None
None
Name
Login ID
Subject
Message No.
Date
Message

(b)

Why would anyone use **Search?** Perhaps your instructor sent you a message on a certain date, and you can't recall what that message said. To access it quickly, **Search** under **Folder,** and you will be able to look for all messages by name, date, or subject.

Understanding Search

Search provides the ability to search all folders and both read and unread messages (Figure WCT 30a). Notice all the drop-down arrows. Click on these to view drop-down menus (Figure WCT 30b).

You can specify whether you want to view the bulletin board with a Full Screen or a Split Screen in the right frame and whether you want the messages to be Threaded or Unthreaded in the listing. Simply access the **Options** menu on the bottom of the left frame and specify **Threaded** or **Unthreaded** and **Full Screen** or **Split Screen.** WebCT will remember your specifications and use them whenever you enter the bulletin board.

Bulletin Board (asynchronous)

The course bulletin board provides a public environment where participants communicate in an *asynchronous* fashion. Participants leave posts (messages) on the bulletin board for others to read and respond to. The bulletin board is an important information source because it provides messages from the instructor as well as questions, answers, and comments from other students.

Notice the two bulletin board icons. Both provide access to the bulletin board and may be located on the same tool pages in your course as the mail icons. The **Bulletins** icon with radiating lines announces there are new messages in the bulletin board. (You will not find this **Bulletins** icon on a lesson's button bar.)

Just as the mail icons access your e-mail, the bulletin-board icons access the public bulletin board. The e-mail and bulletin board interfaces look very much alike because they are both communication tools. Also, like e-mail, the bulletin board interface is arranged in frames.

The Left Frame

- The left frame in the mail interface shows **Folder.** You may sort your mail messages into folders once you read them.
- The left frame in the bulletin board interface shows **Forum** (Figure WCT 31). You place your bulletin-board messages into a forum before you send them.

FIGURE WCT 31
Bulletin Board Left Frame

Home
Help
Compose
Forum
Show All
Catch Up All
Update Listing
Search
Hide Menu
Select All
Select None
Compile
Mark Read
Mark Unread
Move
Delete
Hide Menu
Unthreaded
Full Screen

The Top and Bottom Frames

The top and bottom bulletin-board frames display the listing and the message. Unthreaded messages are arranged chronologically, while threaded messages are indented to indicate the threading (Figure WCT 32). To view all messages to the bulletin board, click on **Show All** in the left frame.

FIGURE WCT 32
Bulletin Board Messages

Welcome! [Forum Main]
☐ 1 Instructor (Mon, Dec. 22, 1997, 14:50)

How to use this forum [Forum Homework Forum]
☐ 2 Instructor (Wed, Sep 2, 1998, 12:22) NEW
☐ 3 Pat Brenner (Wed, Sep 2, 1998, 12:25) NEW
☐ 4 Guest Student (Thu, Sep 24, 1998, 09:24)

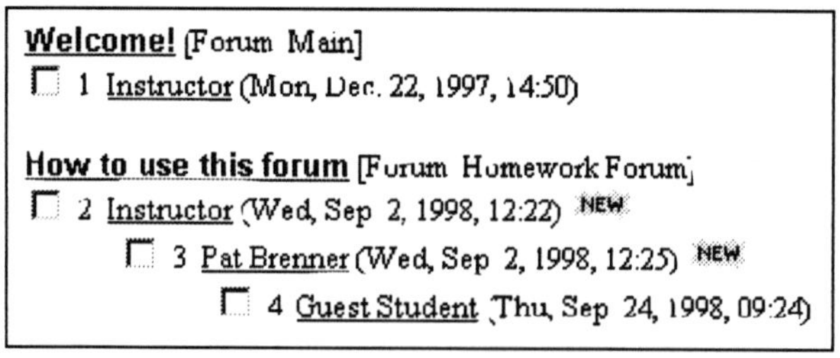

FIGURE WCT 33
Sending E-mail in the Bulletin Board

Mail	Reply	Quote	Save

Privacy Features

Privacy features make mail private, but bulletin-board messages are public. However, you may elect to e-mail a class member in the bulletin-board section by selecting the **Mail** option above the message (Figure WCT 33).

Forum

Notice the first line on the top frame names the Forum being viewed and which messages are being shown (Figure WCT 32). All WebCT courses have three basic forums: All, Main, and Notes.

- **All** contains all posts to the bulletin board and is accessed by selecting **Forum ➤ All.**
- **Main** is the main forum for general discussion. When you access the bulletin board from the course home page (or a subsequent tool page), you enter the **Main** forum. You may elect to post to the **Main** forum, or you may be required to post to a forum created by your instructor. You select the forum to post when you access bulletin board from the **Main** forum.
- **Notes** contains messages specific to a lesson. These posts are threaded according to the title of the lesson. Do not select an alternate forum when you access bulletin board from a lesson. All posts from lessons appear in **Notes.**

If you have a long message to post to the bulletin board and elect not to post the message as an attachment, consider creating it in a word processor and then cutting and pasting the text into the **Compose** text box. This will allow you to think about what you are writing while in the word processor and to save a backup copy for yourself. Keep in mind, though, that when you cut and paste, only the text is picked up; you lose any document formatting you have made.

Any other forums that may appear in your course were created by the instructor to assist in the organization of the bulletin board. If your instructor plans frequent bulletin board communication, he or she may create several different forums, so make sure you are accessing the correct forum.

To post to a forum created by your instructor, follow these instructions:

- Access **Bulletins** from the course home page (or subsequent tool page) and not from the lesson.
- Click on **Compose.** Notice the *Forum:* prompt with the title of the forum and the drop-down menu that reveals all forums (Figure WCT 34). Make sure the forum you wish to post to is selected.

FIGURE WCT 34
Choosing a Forum

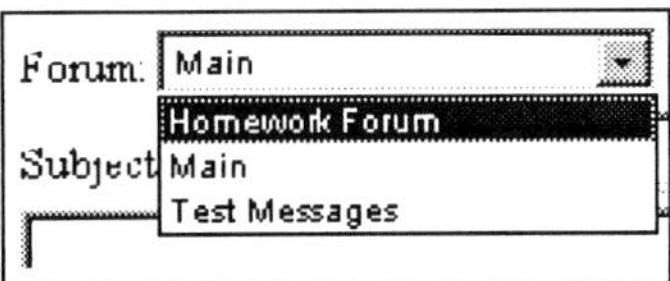

- Continue with the subject line and the text box just as in mail. Notice you may use attachments here, and you may change the size of the text box to accommodate longer messages.

If you wish to attach a document in mail or bulletin board, familiarize yourself with the attachment process.

Sending Attachments in Mail and Bulletin Board

Some documents may be larger than what is comfortable to insert into the text boxes in mail and bulletin board. In these instances you should use an attachment. Perhaps you have noticed the **Attach** button in both the mail and bulletin board **Compose** windows. Clicking on this button activates the attach process.

Attach...

How Your Web Browser Reads Documents

Understanding how your browser reads documents is important to understanding how to attach files to your documents. Your online course takes place in a Web-based environment that is based on HTML, a Web-based language. You may chose to create a document in a word-processing program on your computer, save it as a text file, and attach it to a message. However, you can't be certain that everyone in your online course has software that will read that attachment. You may work on a PC with Word Perfect 8, while a classmate may be working on a Macintosh with ClarisWorks 5.0. These two software programs may not be able to read each other's documents. However, because all participants in your course are working in this Web-based environment, all participants will be able to read HTML documents. It makes sense to save as HTML files all the documents you plan to attach.

Create a course assignment folder on your hard drive or on a floppy disk. Save all your course documents into this folder. You then have a record of all your work. You will be able to (1) upload those document files as attachments when necessary and (2) cut and paste documents when necessary. Keeping copies of your work on your hard drive assures that if your Internet connection shuts down, you will still have a backup copy, and you won't have to start over!

How To Create HTML Files

- Create your files in your word processing program and save them as .HTML files. To do this, you must understand the **Save** feature on your computer. When you save the file the first time, you tell your computer what file type you wish to "save as." Many people just accept the default file type; others recognize that their software program can save a document as a variety of file types. For example, this manual is being written on a PC in Word Perfect 8, and when I save the first time, a window opens like the one in Figure WCT 35a.

  Notice the line that says **File type** (Figure WCT 35b). The arrow on the right indicates that box will reveal a drop-down menu of choices. One of these choices is to save as an .HTML file. Highlight "HTML" so it appears in the box next to **File type.** Save that HTML file into your course assignment folder on your hard drive. Some older word processing programs do not have a "Save as HTML" option. If that is the case, create your document using Web-editing software.

FIGURE WCT 35
Creating an HTML File on a PC

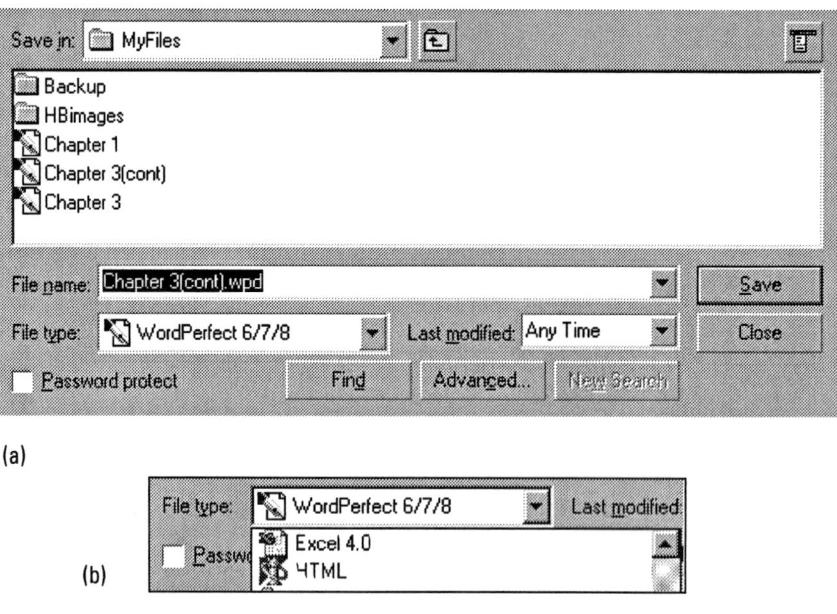

- You can create your documents in Web-editing software. Chances are your Web browser contains a Web editor. In Netscape 4.0, select **File ➤ New ➤ Blank Page,** and you are in Netscape Composer, which is Netscape's Web editor. Here you can work just like you are in a word-processing program, but when you save, you will have an .HTML file that you can attach that everyone in the course will be able to read.

How To Attach a File

The process for attaching files is the same in **mail** and **bulletin board.**

1. Click on **Compose** from the left frame of **mail** or **bulletin board.** Notice the **Attach** button (Figure WCT 36).
2. Click on **Attach** to open the bottom frame that allows you to **Browse** your hard drive to locate the file you wish to attach.
3. Click on **Continue.** If you wish to attach another file, return to the **Attach** button.
4. Click on **Done.**

FIGURE WCT 36
How to Attach a File

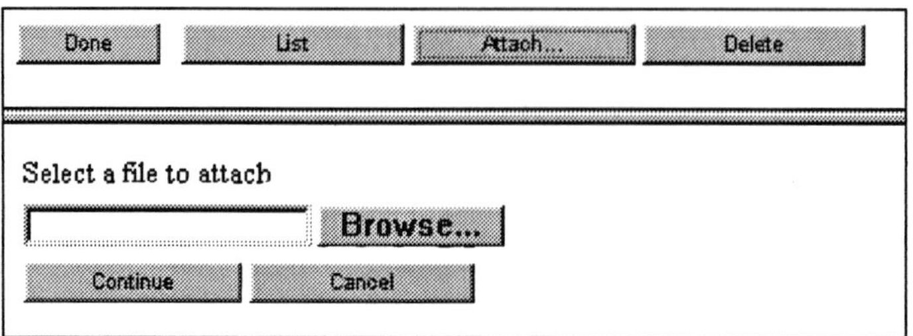

FIGURE WCT 37
Compose Article Window

Compose Article

Post | Preview | Cancel | Don't Wrap | Attach...

Forum: Main

Subject: Lesson One paper

My paper is included in the attachment

5. The **Compose Article** window reappears (Figure WCT 37) for you to select the **Forum** to which you want to post, to enter the **Subject** of your post, and to include a message (which should probably indicate an attachment is included).
6. Click on **Post** (**bulletin boards**) or **Send** (**mail**).

The message and the attachment are then posted to the bulletin board or sent as e-mail.

To Read the Attachment Click on the message and notice the **Attachments** button in the message (Figure WCT 38).

Click on **Attachments,** and the attachment file name in the left frame appears as a link. Click on the text link and the document appears in the right frame (Figure WCT 39).

FIGURE WCT 38
Accessing an Attachment

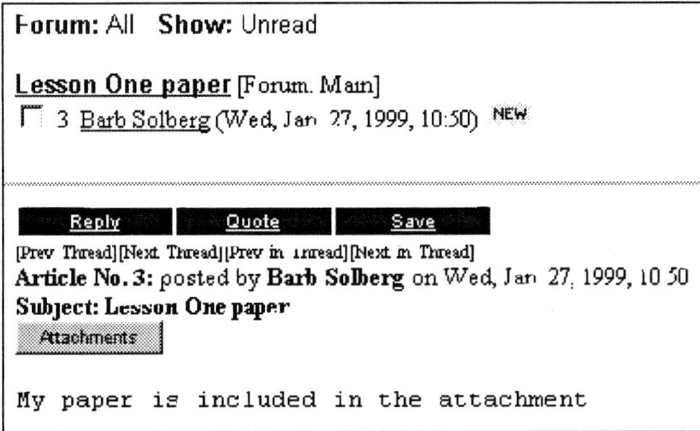

FIGURE WCT 39
Reading the Attachment

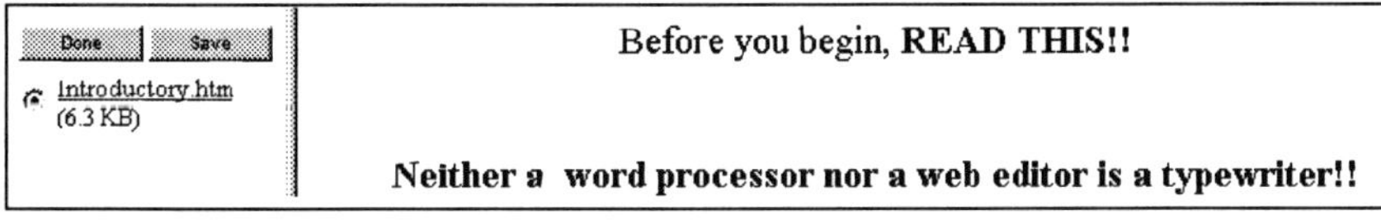

What if I can't access the **Chat** room? Perhaps you are encountering a firewall problem or you haven't set your browser's preferences correctly. In order to use chat, you must have Java enabled and the cache set to reload each time. See the section on "Getting Started: Your Browser."

Chat (synchronous)

The **Chat** icon allows you to access the chat room, where you can have real-time conversations with users of this course or any other WebCT course that resides on the same server. Chat can be used for interactive, online course sessions or for real-time student communication about course projects. Chat offers four general-purpose rooms, one general room for the course, and one room for all courses on the server (Figure WCT 40). Please note that the chat sessions in the four general-purpose rooms are logged. This means that the conversation is recorded in text form and available to the instructor. To enter a room, simply click on it. Clicking on the chat room you desire opens that chat room (Figure WCT 41).

The chat window has three areas:

FIGURE WCT 40
WebCT Chat Room

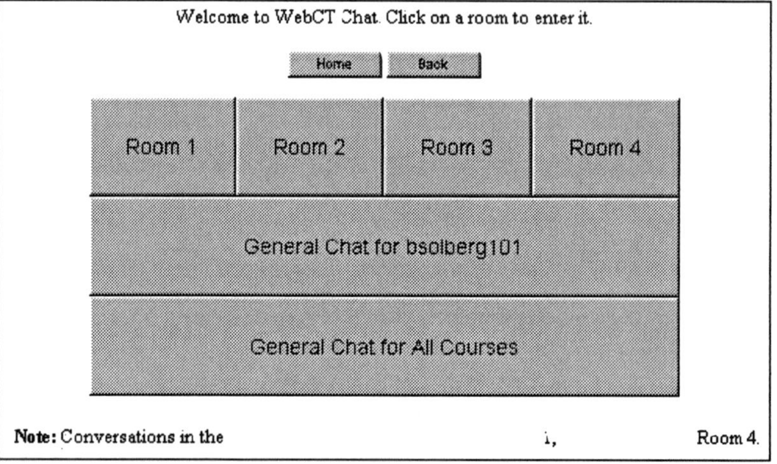

Is it possible to send a private message to someone in the chat room? Yes. In the **Users Logged On** box, click on the name of the person(s) to whom you want to send a private message. The **Shift** and **Control** keys on your keyboard enable certain functions. If you hold down one of them while you click on names, you will see how you can select more than one name. Only those names highlighted will receive your message, and that message will not appear in the chat log. When you want to communicate with the entire group again, click on those names to deselect them.

FIGURE WCT 41
Opening a Chat Room

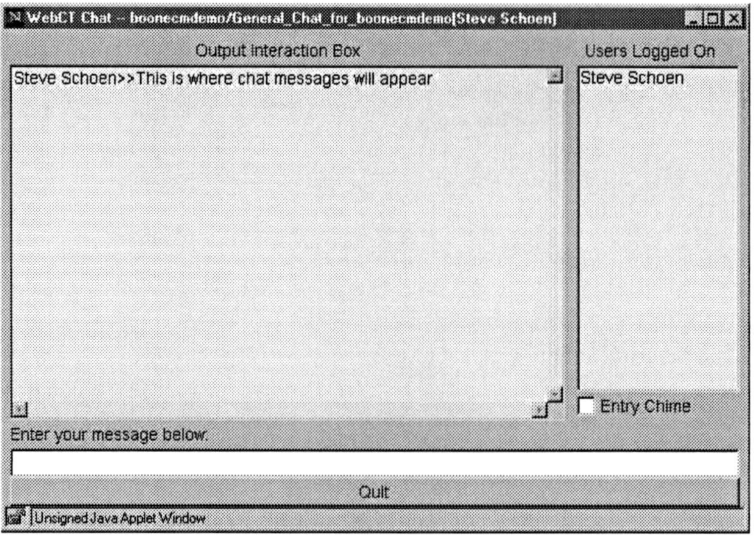

- **Enter your message below** Put your cursor in this text box, type your message, and click **Return** (or **Enter**) on your keyboard
- **Output Interaction** box Once you click **Return** or **Enter,** your message is displayed in this box, along with all other messages sent and received.
- **Users Logged On** The names of all who are currently in the chat room are listed here. If you want to be notified when someone enters the chat room, click on the **Entry Chime** check box. The chime will sound whether you are in chat or are working elsewhere in WebCT. This means you could be working on a lesson, and, when you hear a chime, you know that there is activity in the chat room.

To quit WebCT chat, you must click on the **Quit** bar at the bottom of the chat window.

Home Page and Presentation Tools

Student Home Pages (asynchronous)

Students are able to create home pages in the WebCT course by clicking on the **Student Listing and Home Pages** icon. A window will open with two frames: the left frame contains a list of students in the course, while the right frame is the home page-view frame.

- Each student name is preceded by a mail icon enabling you to send e-mail to that student.
- Students whose names are linked have already created a home page, which you can access by clicking on the student name.
- Your name will always be highlighted for you. Click on your own name to access the home page creation buttons on the right bottom.

Creating Your Home Page WebCT provides the buttons you will use to create your home page (Figure WCT 42). All the files you need (images, backgrounds) must be on your hard drive or a floppy disk. The WebCT student home page designer buttons allow you to access the tools for creating your home page. Click on the WebCT professor icon to open a help window that explains all the tools and how to create your home page. When you have completed your home page, click on **Done** to save your page. Then others in the course may view your home page.

Student Presentations (asynchronous)

The WebCT **Student Presentations** tool allows you to place documents into the course for your instructor and other students to view. Before you can place a document into **Student Presentations,** that document must be created.

FIGURE WCT 42
Creating a Student Home Page

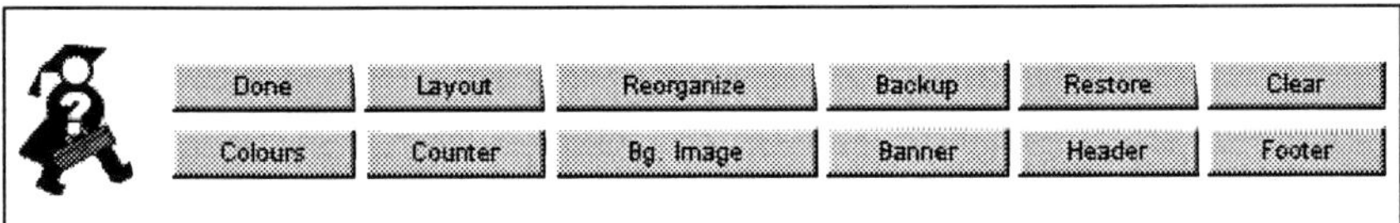

How To Create a Document for Student Presentations:

- Create a folder on your hard drive or floppy disk and call it Student Presentations. Save all student presentation documents and images into this folder.
- Create the document in a Web-editing program like Netscape Composer or in a word-processing program that will allow you to save documents as .HTML files. The lead document must be saved as "index.html." If you forget to save as index.html, specific WebCT buttons available in this module will allow you to rename the file.

You may want to find a guide to creating Web pages to learn how to create a good Web site for your presentation.

How To Upload Files or Images into Student Presentations Access the presentation tool by clicking on the **Presentations** icon usually found on one of the course tool pages. The browser window divides into upper and lower frames (Figure WCT 43). These frames display

- Buttons to return to the home page (**Home**) and to move **Back** one page.
- A reminder to rename the lead file "index.html"
- A **Mail** link to the group members in each group. If the group contains multiple members, **Mail** will link to all group members.
- A link to the **Group.** Clicking on **Group** will open the bottom frame to reveal the names of **Group Members.**
- An **[Edit Files]** link for students in the named group. Clicking on this link provides the features necessary to upload and to edit the presentation.
- A link to the group **Project.** Those projects that have been uploaded into presentations will be linked as in the image. Those groups that have not yet uploaded a presentation will not have a link. Clicking on the linked project title opens the project in a new window.

FIGURE WCT 43
Student Presentations

Student Presentations

Home Back

NOTE: Please remember to rename your starting file to **index.html**

Mail	Group	Project
	Group One [Edit Files]	None
	Group Two	None

Group Members

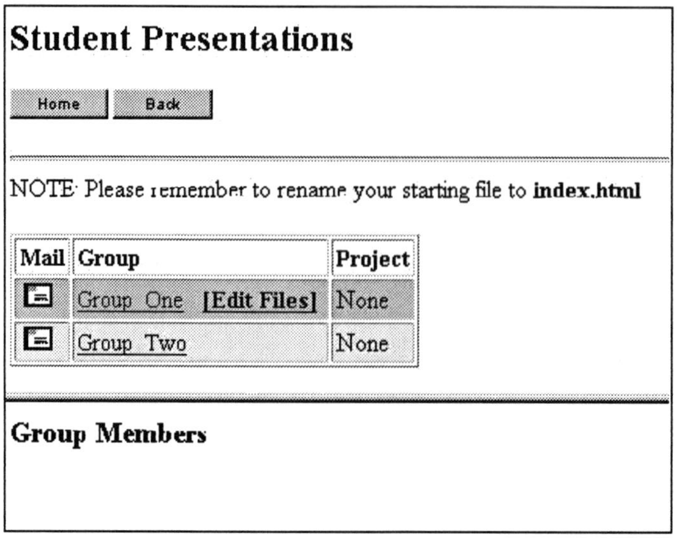

FIGURE WCT 44
Presentation-Design Tools

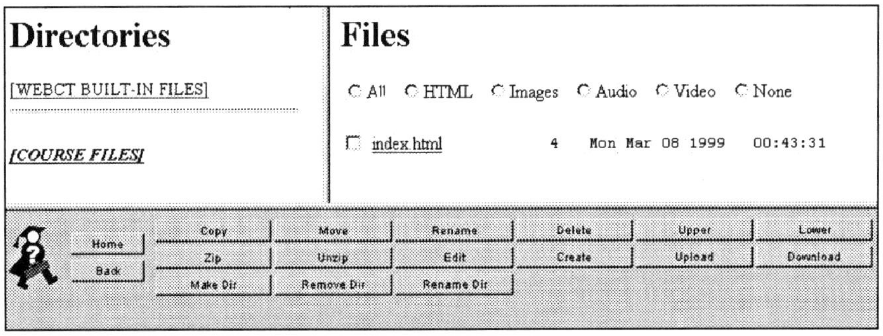

How To Upload Your Presentation WebCT automatically inserts the **[Edit Files]** link next to the group to which you belong. This gives you rights to make changes to your group presentation. Clicking on the **[Edit Files]** link will open presentation-design tools for your use (Figure WCT 44).

Clicking on the WebCT professor will give you access to instructions for the buttons you have available. Understanding **Rename, Delete, Unzip, Edit, Upload, Download** will be most beneficial to you.

- **Rename** allows you to rename your file to "index.html" if you forgot to name the file as index.html.
- **Delete** allows you to delete a file from the directory. This is helpful should you decide to remove the presentation and try again!
- **Unzip** allows you to unzip a compressed file.
- **Edit** allows you to edit a file. Put a checkmark in the box next to the .HTML file you wish to edit. Two frames will open. The right frame will show the file in HTML code. You can edit here if you feel confident reading the HTML code.

  If you don't feel confident in HTML code, perhaps you should download the file to your hard drive and edit it with HTML-editing software. Click on the file you wish to download, then click on **Download** to save the file to your hard drive. Edit it there, save it, and then upload it, writing over the original file.
- **Upload** opens a window for browsing your hard drive or floppy diskette to access your presentation file. Locate your presentation file and click on **Continue** until your presentation file's name appears in the **File** frame.

Taking Tests

Your online instructor may elect to give online course examinations. These online quizzes, tests, or exams (these terms are often used interchangeably) may

- Be set to be taken on a certain date
- Be timed
- Be taken a specified number of times, up to five times
- Contain multiple-choice, true/false, matching, short answer, calculated, or paragraph questions

- Be automatically scored by WebCT or, in the case of paragraph answers, by the instructor or a grader
- Be set so you can review your test results

Because all these options exist, it is important for you to read all the instructions prior to taking the quiz.

Online quizzes may be accessed in one of two ways depending on how your online instructor chooses to deliver them.

1. The **Quiz** icon may be on the home page or a subsequent tool page.
2. The **Quiz** icon may be on the button bar for the specific lesson.

Accessing Quizzes and Exams from the Quiz Home Page

If the **Quiz** icon is on the home page or an additional tool page, click on the icon to access the Quiz Home Page (Figure WCT 45). For each quiz listed, the following information is given:

- **Title** offers access to the specific quiz. If the quiz is not yet available or if you have taken the quiz the maximum number of times, the title will not be linked.
- **Availability** shows the time period in which the test may be accessed.
- **Duration** shows the time allotted for taking the quiz.
- **Grade** indicates the number of points you received out of total points possible.
- **Tries** shows the number of times you attempted the quiz along with the maximum number of tries allowed. Once you have taken a quiz, you will see the number of tries out of the total as in "Tries: 1/5 [1]." The bracketed number links to that attempt so you can view that quiz and your answers. Your online instructor may also elect to show you the correct answers or to allow you to retake that quiz and have it regraded.

Click on the quiz title to access that quiz. The screen divides into two frames.

1. The left frame reveals the test questions with a scroll bar on the right of that frame to display all questions (Figure WCT 46). This frame also reveals
   - The name of the quiz
   - Your name
   - The number of questions

FIGURE WCT 45
Quiz Home Page

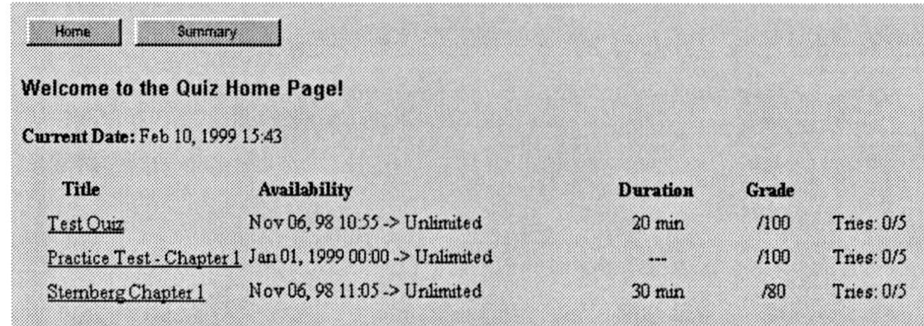

FIGURE WCT 46
Left and Right Frames of Quiz

Test Quiz
Name: Steve Schoen
Start Time: Mar 10, 1999 13:02 Time Allowed: 20 min
Number of Questions: 4

Time remaining: 20 min.
Unanswered
Answered
1 2 3 4

(a)

Question 1 (25 points)

The term e-mail means

1 "easy" mail
2. "elitist" mail
3 "electronic" mail
4 "evolutionary" mail

Save Answer

Unanswered
Answered
1 2 3 4

(b)

> If you start a quiz and decide to peek at the questions and then back out without taking the quiz, your instructor will be notified that you are "In Progress." If the quiz can be taken only once, backing out without taking the quiz will not extend the time allotted for the quiz! You will probably make a zero on the test. If the test can be taken more than once, note that. Take the quiz the first time, click on **Finish,** and then return to take it a second time when you feel more confident.

> Always be certain to always note how many times you can take a test and how long you have to take the test. Do not forget to click on **Save Answer** and **Finish.**

- **Finish** and **Help** buttons (click on **Finish** when you complete the quiz, **Help** if you need help)
- Introductory test information provided by your instructor

2. The right frame contains a table that lists which questions have and have not been answered. A red bullet indicates an unanswered question, while a green star indicates that the question has been answered. Clicking on **Save Answer** under each question (Figure WCT 46b) will record your answer and turn the red bullet into a green star.

Finish

When you have finished the quiz, be sure to click on **Finish.** If you have not completed all the questions, a window will appear listing the questions you have not completed. You will be able to return to finish the questions you missed or move on. Moving on will open a dialog box that asks if you are ready to submit the quiz for grading (Figure WCT 47a). Click on **OK** and you'll get the choices shown in Figure WCT 47b: going to the home page **(Home),** going **Back**, or going to **View Results** of the test (if your instructor has released scores).

FIGURE WCT 47
Right Frame of Quiz

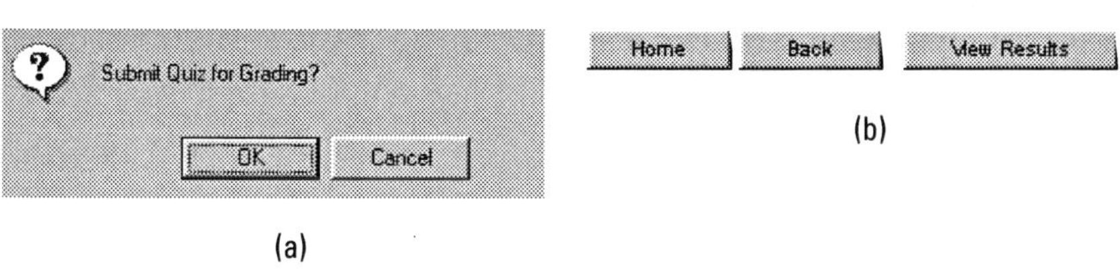

(a) (b)

FIGURE WCT 48
View Results

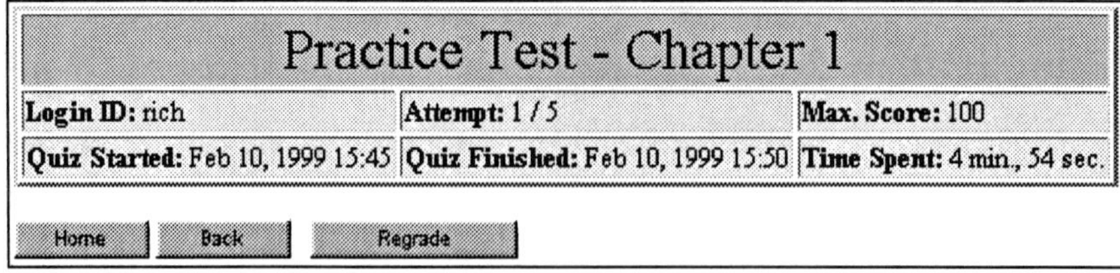

View Results opens a window (Figure WCT 48) that reports how many attempts you made at the quiz, your maximum score, when you took the quiz, and time spent. The instructor can set the quiz to be taken multiple times if he or she chooses.

Accessing Quiz from the Lesson's Button Bar

If the instructor elected to insert the quiz from the lesson, you will see the **Quiz** icon on the lesson button bar. Clicking on that icon reveals a window like the one in Figure WCT 49 with the test title, availability, and number of attempts. Click on the linked quiz title and follow the same instructions as accessing quizzes from the Quiz Home Page.

Checking Your Progress

Most students are interested in their progress in a course. You can get this information by using the **My Progress** and **My Record** buttons. both in terms of how much of the course they've covered and what their grades are.

My Progress

Clicking on the **My Progress** icon will provide some pretty revealing information! You will be able to see

- When you first accessed the course
- When you last accessed the course

FIGURE WCT 49
Accessing the Quiz from the Lesson Button Bar

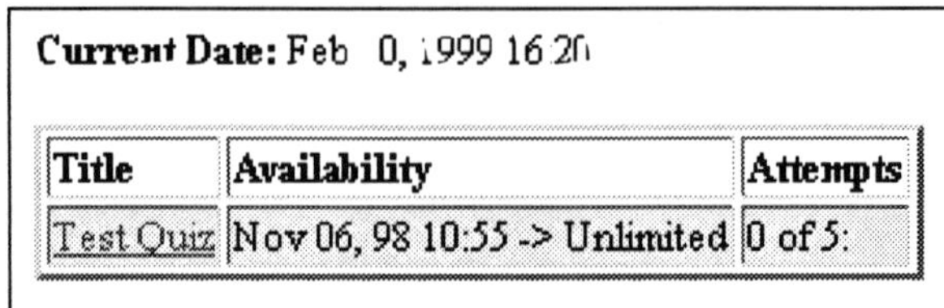
Current Date: Feb 0, 1999 16 2

Title	Availability	Attempts
Test Quiz	Nov 06, 98 10:55 -> Unlimited	0 of 5:

- The name of the last page you visited
- How much of the course you have visited

Remember that this information is also available to your instructor. Clicking the **My Progress** icon opens a window similar to the one in Figure WCT 50. Notice the five gray buttons below the words "Student Profile." Clicking on these buttons reveals information about your distribution, coverage, and history in the course.

- **Distribution** reveals how many times you have clicked on parts of the course including the home page, content pages, glossary, goals, references, etc. Both you and your instructor have access to how information about much of the course you have accessed.
- **Coverage** reveals how much of the course you have accessed in terms of pages and percentage of entire course (Figure WCT 51).
- **History** reveals not only the pages accessed but also the time of access (Figure WCT 52). Your instructor also has access to statistics on how much time you spent on each page. When you view successive pages of content, you can use the history feature to review how much time you spent on each page of content.

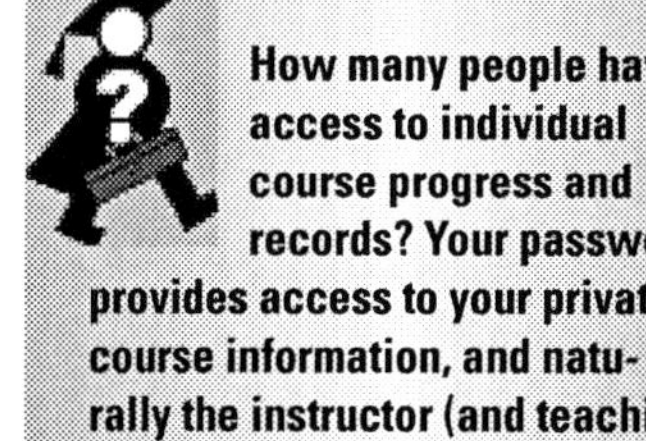

How many people have access to individual course progress and records? Your password provides access to your private course information, and naturally the instructor (and teaching assistant) has access to all students' progress and grades. You can access only your own information.

FIGURE WCT 50
Student Profile Window

Student Profile

Home | Back | Distribution | Coverage | History

Full name: Steve Schoen — Login ID: sschoen
First login: Fri Jan 22 17:50:05 1999 — Last login: Wed Mar 10 14:02:23 1999
Total number of accesses: 45 — Last page visited: Chapter 2: Creating Value through Customer Satisfaction

Distribution of Hits for Steve Schoen

Page	Hits
Homepage	11
Tool Pages	10
Content Pages	12
Glossary	6
Goals	1

FIGURE WCT 51
Coverage of the Course

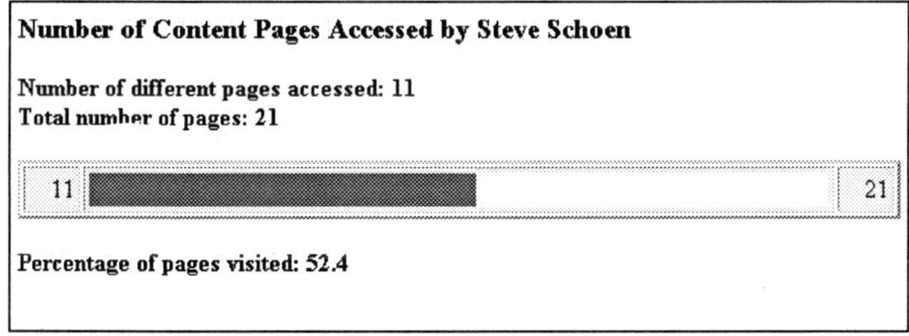

FIGURE WCT 52
History of Pages Visited

History of Pages Visited by Steve Schoen

[Prev 10 Accesses] [Next 10 Accesses]

	Page Name	Time of Access
12	Chapter 2: Creating Value through Customer Satisfaction and Quality	Wed Mar 10 13:56:20 1999
11	Three Reasons for Studying Marketing	Wed Mar 10 13:55:59 1999
10	Ethical Practices	Wed Mar 10 13:55:17 1999
9	The Universal Functions	Wed Mar 10 13:54:43 1999
8	Marketing Environment	Wed Mar 10 13:53:25 1999
7	Marketing Strategy	Wed Mar 10 13:52:08 1999
6	Nontraditional Marketing	Wed Mar 10 13:50:48 1999

My Record

The **My Record** icon will reveal your grades in the course. If you have taken online tests or if the instructor has given other grades and inserted them into this online record, you will see your grades.

FIGURE WCT 53
Student Record

Current Student Record for sschoen

Home | Back

First Name	Last Name	Login ID	Student No	Midterm	Final Exam	Final Grade /
Steve	Schoen	sschoen	001	85	93	--

Click on a column title to see statistics (if available).

SUMMARY

WebCT—World Wide **Web** Course **T**ools—is online course management software that resides on a Web server and can be used by anyone with a computer and World Wide Web access. WebCT courses are password-protected for both student and instructor privacy. Just about everything needed for distance learning is available in a WebCT course including lessons, communication environments like private e-mail, bulletin board, chat, student presentation and home page areas, and those typical course accessories like a glossary, index, references, and lesson objectives. In WebCT students may also take self tests to check their learning in a non-graded environment. Online graded quizzes can include multiple choice, matching, short answer, calculated, and paragraph-type questions.

Students who spend the first few days of the course familiarizing themselves with WebCT will gain confidence quickly. The WebCT guide provides valuable information on WebCT tools and environments in addition to providing valuable tips for online students and answers to questions students might want to ask their WebCT instructor.

Because the world of online education is relatively new, both student and instructor are probably still learning to use this new environment. To succeed, both student and instructor will need to keep communication lines open, establish a regular online course schedule, and participate in the communication environments appropriately and regularly. The Internet has changed and will continue to change how we live, how we do business, how we communicate, and how we learn. As an online student, you are a pioneer! Good luck in your new adventure.

KEY TERMS

Attach a file (WCT 28-29)
Bookmark (WCT 7)
Bulletin Board (WCT 25-27)
Button bar (WCT 14)
Cache (WCT 7)
Calendar (WCT 13)
Compile lessons (WCT 18)
Chat (WCT 30)
Change your password (WCT 18)
Compose a message (WCT 23)
Folders (WCT 23-24)
Forward a message (WCT 23)
Forum (WCT 26-27)
Glossary (WCT 14-15)
Goals (WCT 16)
Home Page (WCT 13)
HTML files (WCT 27-28
Index (WCT 16))
Logging on (WCT 5)
Mail (WCT 19-25)
Memory (WCT 4)
My Notes (WCT 17)
My Progress (WCT 36-37)
My Record (WCT 38)
Navigational tools (WCT 14)
Operating system (OS) (WCT 3)
Output Interaction box (WCT 31)
Plug-ins (WCT 7)
Preferences (WCT 12)
Private mail (WCT 19)
Properties (WCT 12)
RAM (WCT 4)
References (WCT 16)
Refresh (WCT 14)
Retrace (WCT 14)
Resume Session (WCT 18)
Search the course (WCT 16)
Self Test (WCT 17)
Student Home Pages (WCT 31)
Student Presentations (WCT 31-33)
Taking tests (WCT 33-36)
Thread (WCT 20)
Tips (WCT 10-12)
Troubleshooting (WCT 8-10)
Uploading files or images (WCT 32)
Uploading your presentations (WCT 33)